T0285590

Praise for
Healing HEALTHCARE

"This is a beacon of hope for our ailing healthcare system! *Healing Healthcare* unveils the urgent necessity of prioritizing workforce well-being. Going beyond patient care, it celebrates the fortitude of frontline caregivers, spotlighting nurses. Drawing from diverse voices, it provides actionable strategies and compelling narratives, paving the way for a genuinely healed and resilient healthcare landscape. This is an excellent evidence-based approach to solving an important issue."

DR. RICHARD A. CHAIFETZ, founder, chair, and CEO of ComPsych

"Act now and secure your copy of this impactful book by Sharon and Dina! In the urgent realm of *Healing Healthcare*, the authors provide timely strategies for today's challenges. As a health executive, I witness the real struggles of healthcare staff, and this book is a crucial catalyst for addressing well-being and creating a psychologically safe environment. Don't miss the opportunity to shape the future of our profession."

LISA LOCHNER, president, Missouri Baptist Sullivan Hospital

"*Healing Healthcare* employs gripping stories from twenty-eight nationally recognized contributing authors. Like the authors, the book is remarkable for its wisdom, insight, and honesty in describing solutions for workforce challenges, struggles for well-being, and the knowledge needed for reform. It is a compelling journey of resilience and transformation . . . a must-read."

DONNA HILL HOWES, senior vice president and chief nursing officer, Sharecare

"*Healing Healthcare* is a transformative journey for the healthcare landscape. With stories from known healthcare leaders, it unveils the stark truths of a broken system. With evidence-based strategies shared by twenty-eight contributors, this book is a captivating invitation to action for leaders and practitioners ready to repair our healthcare system, fostering a future of resilience, respect, and a positive cultural position for communities and the population. An essential read and blueprint for the future of healthcare!"

> **NANCY ROLLINS GANTZ**, PhD, RN, MBA, MSN, CNEn, CGNC, FFNMRCSI, FAONL, secretary, Sigma Theta Tau International Honor Society of Nursing

"It will take HEART change and LOVING evidence-based right action to heal healthcare. It will require that we drive out fear and build trust. It will necessitate high-integrity people leading, serving, loving, and teaching. *Healing Healthcare* delivers. Brilliant, caring leaders providing tangible and inspirational wisdom positioning all to heal healthcare."

> **TOM DAHLBORG**, president and CEO, Dahlborg HealthCARING Leadership Group, LLC (DHLG)

"Insight, creativity, and action. Sharon Weinstein and Dina Readinger are on a quest to heal healthcare. In their new book, *Healing Healthcare: Evidence-Based Strategies to Mend Our Broken System*, the authors introduce us to the Diagnostic Design Thinking Group Process, demonstrating its application to shifting from current 'problems' to desired 'outcomes.' Addressing workforce and well-being challenges, they invite leaders to create the future and think differently by design. If you are looking for strategies to mend a broken healthcare system, add this book to your reading list and reflect on the wisdom, insight, creativity, and actions offered by the authors and contributors."

> **DANIEL J. PESUT**, PhD, RN, FAAN, emeritus professor, University of Minnesota and Indiana University Schools of Nursing

"Embark on a transformative journey with *Healing Healthcare*, where pioneering nursing leaders utilize a Diagnostic Design Thinking model that offers concrete, evidence-based solutions to revolutionize our healthcare landscape. Get ready to delve into workforce challenges, struggles for well-being, and wisdom required for reform."

MARK MURAWSKI, MBA, director of contract services, Bayer US Pharmaceuticals and Bayer US; cochair, Healthcare Businesswomen's Association Partnership Committee

"*Healing Healthcare* is your indispensable toolkit for fostering an inclusive and psychologically safe post-pandemic environment. Dive into this book to uncover evidence-based strategies tailored for you, your team, and your organization."

SUSAN KEANE BAKER, MHA, author of *Split-Second Kindness: Making a Difference When Time is Limited*

"In their valuable new book, Sharon Weinstein and Dina Readinger have assembled a cadre of healthcare experts to provide targeted strategies for addressing the issues in our healthcare system. With over four decades of experience collaborating with home health, hospice, and home care leaders, I'm enthusiastic about the fresh perspectives and innovative ideas they bring to our healthcare segment. It's a must-read for every leader of a healthcare organization and policymakers alike."

STEPHEN TWEED, CEO, Leading Home Care . . . a Tweed Jeffries Company; founder, Home Care CEO Forum

www.amplifypublishinggroup.com

Healing Healthcare: Evidence-Based Strategies to Mend Our Broken System

**Special thanks to Kimb Williams for designing the interior tables and for
consulting on the cover design.**

For more information, please contact:
Amplify Publishing, an imprint of Amplify Publishing Group
620 Herndon Parkway, Suite 220
Herndon, VA 20170
info@amplifypublishing.com

Library of Congress Control Number: 2023923190

CPSIA Code: PRV0624A

ISBN-13: 978-1-63755-966-6

Printed in the United States

Bernadette Melnyk once said, "It is the CNOs who get the applause . . . frontline nurses deserve the standing ovation!"

Nurses truly deserve a standing ovation; their herculean efforts have brought us this far . . . both during and since the pandemic. Vanderbilt University Medical Center unveiled a mural in honor of National Nurses Week in 2021. Other hospitals and health systems have honored nurses and nursing in their own ways.[1] This book is our contribution to that ovation.

From Sharon M. Weinstein
As a nurse, I take pride in my chosen profession. It is a privilege to collaborate with a team of contributing authors who share the joy in the journey. This book is the result of your commitment to the profession, to those for whom we care, and those we teach across the country and around the globe.

I am grateful for a family that appreciates my calling. They have supported my travels, my passion for continuous learning, and a profession that knows no limits.

To my brilliant coauthor and business partner, Dina Readinger, thank you for the privilege of collaborating with you. You are a beacon of light!

Consider this book a "gratitude" journal, one that includes content from great minds within the profession. Their reflections celebrate our past and inspire our future.

From Dina Readinger
To the nurses who selflessly give of themselves and to others, and to our friends and our families—we hear you!

To Sharon Weinstein, my business partner, who spent endless hours editing, coordinating, and ensuring this book gets published—thank you! Your work is a gift of love. May we continue our mission: teaching others to Think Differently!

Sharon M. Weinstein & Dina Readinger

Healing
HEALTHCARE

Evidence-Based Strategies
to Mend Our Broken System

amplify
an imprint of Amplify Publishing Group

Contents

Foreword

Bernadette Mazurek Melnyk

PhD, APRN-CNP, EBP-C, FAANP, FNAP, FAAN;
Vice President for Health Promotion and Chief Wellness Officer,
The Ohio State University;
Helene Fuld Health Trust Professor of Evidence-Based Practice;
Executive Director of the Helene Fuld Health Trust Institute for Evidence-
Based Practice in Nursing and Healthcare;
Former Dean, College of Nursing;
Professor of Pediatrics and Psychiatry, College of Medicine

There is currently a perfect dark storm in healthcare. Levels of burnout, depression, and suicide in clinicians are at epidemic levels throughout the nation, adversely affecting the quality and safety of healthcare. It has been well established through multiple studies that caring clinicians who are burned out make more medical errors, resulting in hundreds of thousands of patients unnecessarily dying every year in the United States. The tremendous strain, moral distress, and overwhelming stressors brought on by the COVID-19 pandemic, including high acuity of patients, increased caseloads, and staffing shortages, have led to the ongoing great resignation as more nurses and physicians are choosing to leave the workforce. System issues that cause burnout (e.g., work overload, understaffing, unnecessary tasks, ineffective teamwork, and problems with the electronic health record) must be fixed, and institutions must invest in building wellness cultures in which people feel cared about and valued. Institutions also must provide evidence-based wellness programming, services, and resources that optimize the health and well-being of their workforce, which will improve healthcare quality and safety.

Unfortunately, we are living in a sick and crisis-care health system. Although we will always need great sick and crisis care, we must shift our current paradigm to one of wellness and prevention if our population's health outcomes are to improve. We know what works to improve the health and well-being of nurses, the healthcare workforce, nursing students, and our patients, but it typically takes fifteen years or longer to translate findings from research and evidence-based recommendations into real-world clinical and academic settings and improved outcomes. We cannot wait decades to implement best evidence in our healthcare systems and academic institutions to improve the health and lives of our frontline nurses, our students, and our patients. The time for urgent action is NOW!

Sharon Weinstein and Dina Readinger have created a "must-have" book that is packed full of evidence-based strategies and insights from nationally recognized leaders who offer their expertise, stories, and wisdom on how to improve the current state of healthcare and strategies to enhance the health and well-being of nurses. Each chapter provides practical advice and offers "golden nuggets" that can be readily implemented in the real world in an easy-to-read format. This book should be a staple of everyone's resources.

Foreword

Katie Boston-Leary

PhD, MBA, MHA, RN, NEA-BC
Director of Nursing Programs, American Nurses Association
Adjunct Professor, University of Maryland School of Nursing
Past President, Maryland Organization of Nurse Leaders

Nurses are the foundation, the cornerstones, the brick and mortar, and the shining light of every healthcare system in the United States and around the world, but we humbly recognize that we cannot do it alone. We need our partners in delivering excellent care. We have a social contract and a moral obligation to meet people where they are to get them over the wall of disease and on a steady path to wellness.

At the same time, we have many challenges that make us want to give up fighting for improvements and settle into apathy. For years we didn't do enough to address the human side of nursing. We focused on that perspective for our patients, but not for ourselves. As nurses, we must continually remind ourselves that we deserve happiness, joy, contentment, self-actualization, and human flourishing. Admittedly, this is challenging—we get pulled in so many directions and into so many situations that do not feed our souls and drained spirits.

Healthy Nurse, Healthy Nation is a free online community that provides resources to improve nurses' overall health and well-being. The six domains of well-being are the areas of nutrition, sleep, physical activity, safety, quality of life, and mental health. Healthy nurses beget healthy systems for patients to receive optimal (not just safe) care. The days of striving for outcomes at the expense of nurses' health and well-being should be long gone; that approach is derived from the early industrial age that our forebears and mothers endured. We are either in the Fourth Industrial Revolution or Information Age—what is required from leaders and teams is new, different, and admittedly uncomfortable. Engagement needs to occur in the form of listening, hearing, responding, and closing the loop—essential components to leading today's workers and teams.

So, are we ready for change? A study we conducted in 2023 with Studer and Joslin Insight[1] shows that, in nursing and healthcare, attitudes of neutrality and unwillingness to change outweigh the will to innovate. Why? Unwillingness to change can be rooted in apathy or in the fear of something new or different. We must explore ways to address that issue, because the price we are paying for old processes, policies, procedures, and pathways to delivering care is too high. The new and emerging reality is here, so let's face it. Head on. Eyes wide. Shoulders square. Now charge! And remember to not look back.

Look ahead and start right here!

Introduction

We talk a lot about the pandemic and the impact of its aftermath on our healthcare system. But our system, although revered as one of the best in the world, has been broken for much longer than three years. When COVID-19 cases exploded from coast to coast, healthcare professionals formed a disease-fighting community to facilitate testing, treatment, and the creation and distribution of vaccines. Millions of Americans followed the evidence by donning masks, practicing social distancing, upping their hygiene, and proactively getting tested.

Even before the pandemic, much was being written[1] about the need to maximize value for patients, that is, achieving the best outcome at the lowest cost. Pilot projects in value-based care speak to their efficacy—but isn't the real value in asking the right questions and solving the right problems? The first step toward progress is to define a goal, and the goal for healthcare reform must address more than access, cost containment, profit margins . . . and, yes, more than the patient experience. While a patient's experience is a critical driver of outcomes, the overarching goal must include the forefront of care—those at the bedside.

As the largest group of healthcare professionals in all corners of the world, nurses are the backbone of every healthcare system. And yet, when discussions turn to ways we can restore care, improve the system, and transform health, little mention is made of these professionals, the ones who support the public around the world, providing care, education, and advocacy. In the words of President Barack Obama, "America's nurses are the beating heart of our medical system." The nurses need to be heard!

Our goal in creating *Healing Healthcare* was to supply nurse leaders with an opportunity to be heard, express their opinions, share ideas, and tell their stories. We heard a plethora of tales from so many past and current healthcare leaders—of frustration, cultural misalignment, lack of recognition, pain, and uncertainty. We have tried to capture these anecdotes from the front line, so that we might share them with the greater nursing and healthcare communities and think differently about what's next! You will see that we have divided the book into three primary sections, and they are: Workforce, Well-Being, and Wisdom. The content in each section offers actionable steps and vetted solutions for mending our broken healthcare system!

The Diagnostic Design Thinking Group Process

A Diagnostic Design Thinking Group (DDTG) offers an opportunity for us to think differently in a psychologically safe setting. We ask ourselves who is experiencing the problem, what the problem is (based on observations), what's in the way, where the problem presents itself (and whether others are involved), and finally, why it matters (what value a solution would bring to the user or the system).

Participants in a DDTG each state provocative questions, and group members vote on a question to solve. They then ask non-leading questions that take us to a deeper question or reveal a need for clarity. By tracking ideas, unpacking bottlenecks, and identifying the emotions below the surface, we then restate what was heard to ensure that interpretations are correct. Each member then offers ideas for solving what has become the "right problem," leveraging their own thoughts and experiences.

Examine Figure 1, which depicts the steps in our model. This simple design has brought significant changes in process and profits to organizations large and small.

Such is the model for this book. The benefits of a DDTG are many. A DDTG develops strong social and emotional awareness for leaders and staff; creates psychological safety for the change needed in healthcare today; develops Diagnostic Design Thinking, where solving the right

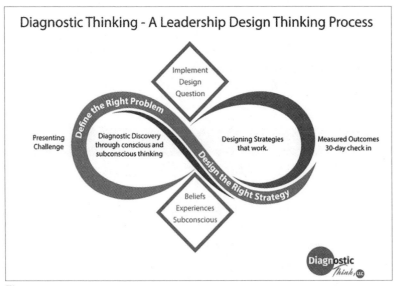

Figure 1

problems leads to better outcomes; creates retention and recruitment strategies; and heals broken systems plagued by noncollaboration.

We have been privileged to lead multiple global groups of professionals through the DDTG process. Through DDTG, we have pinpointed the cost of noncollaboration among many teams. Noncollaboration is a non-win that costs money and reduces profits. See Figure 2.

Why does noncollaboration occur?

- Lack of shared vision.
- Lack of action on the right problem (or any problem at all).
- Lack of transparency and open dialogue with the people who are doing the day-to-day work.
- Employees fear speaking up due to the potential impact on their careers. They don't feel safe sharing their ideas and experiences.

Cost Analysis of Noncollaboration

Cost of noncollaboration depends on various factors of which may be quantitative, but typically subjective and not easily quantifiable. Estimating a financial value is difficult, yet we can provide a general direction of cost and revenue/profit impact.

Examples of Variables and Scenarios	Cost Impact	Revenue/Profit Impact
Inefficiencies or under utilization of resources		
Knowledge transfer delays		
Employee retention, incentives, motivation	↑	↓
Employee turnover, incremental recruiting costs		
Customer satisfaction - Potential New Market Entry		
Product Quality - Risk of lower quality		

Figure 2

Revenue & Profit Projections
Using Generic Assumptions

	Base Scenario	1 Yr Launch Delay	2 Yr Launch Delay
Revenue ($)	2,500M	2,200M	1,600M
Net Profit	20%	13%	4%
Loss in Revenue	N/A	14%	36%
Decline in Net Profit	N/A	8%	17%

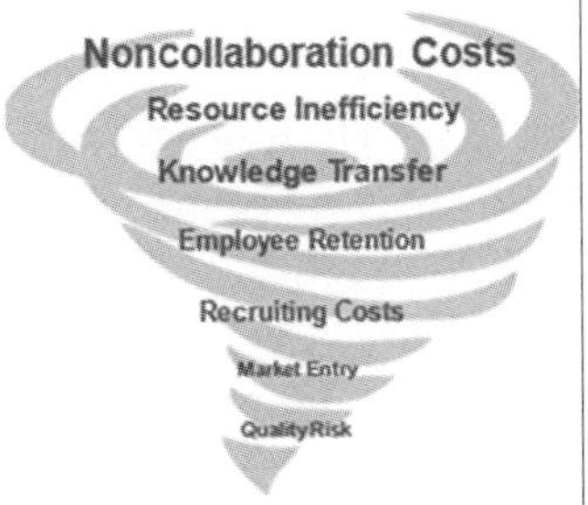

- Noncollaboration will generally lead to launch delays
- Launch delays negatively impact revenue and net profits

Figure 3

A recent study with leaders within a large healthcare organization found it challenged by the lack of cross-functional leadership needed to move the business forward. This led to noncollaboration and a landslide of bad behaviors. We had leaders who were challenged with noncollaboration create a map of influence within their organizations. Each leader reached out to selected individuals to gain their insight and to see if they were aware of the noncollaboration and the costs associated therewith. The leaders then engaged the help of their financial colleagues to address the assumptions that came out of the DDTG session. The evidence was clear: noncollaboration had a negative impact on the bottom line. See Figure 3.

Our Wish for You . . .

In *Healing Healthcare*, we have assembled a group of nurse leaders to answer the right questions. What better time than now to bring these golden nuggets of wisdom directly from their mouths to the public and our greater healthcare community? The narratives of these lived experiences are essential to share and preserve! They hold the key to our future.

This book is intended to be the voice of the unspoken, a call to action for healthcare leaders, and a tool to awaken the sleeping giant: our broken healthcare system. We are on a mission to create a resource for healthcare systems, current and future healthcare leaders (including current frontline nurses), and especially the nurses of the future.

The *Clinician of the Future 2023: Education Edition* reveals the alarming statistic that 23 percent of medical and nursing students in the US are already considering quitting their undergraduate studies. Why? Because they are truly concerned about their mental well-being (60 percent) and the inevitability of burnout (62 percent).[2] The suicide rate for physicians is around 12 percent, and the nurse suicide rate is 18 percent higher than the general population.[3] Multidisciplinary members of the healthcare team have been suffering in silence for decades, and now the world is faced with the realization that our current state of affairs may not be fixable. Nurses remain the backbone of healthcare, and little has been done or even studied to remedy a system in crisis. If this is not addressed now, humankind will suffer.

This book is packed with solutions to the problems that plague our healthcare systems today—the problems that lead to these troubling sentiments among prospective nurses. Nurse leaders share their experiences, thoughts, evidence, and strategies to ensure the health of our healthcare. What you will find within are actionable steps for fixing a system that is currently suffering in silence. We must get this book into the hands of those making the decisions. Together we can be the difference and a voice for change. May we wake this sleeping giant.

Part One
Workforce

"Although your educational journey may be difficult at times, you will reap the reward of utmost satisfaction when holding your nursing diploma for the first time— and nothing will ever compare to the fulfillment that improving and saving the lives of others will bring!"

–Mikhail Shneyder,
Nightingale College president and CEO

C lose your eyes and reflect on the first day you stepped into the role of a registered nurse (RN). You had arrived, and you were going to make a difference. You would join a workforce of like-minded peers with a passion for human well-being and the restoration of health. We believe that every nurse, regardless of where they were educated, has experienced this passion—the rewards that come from knowing that you have and will continue to affect the lifespan of citizens across the globe. This is nursing; this is what brought us to this place, and until now, has driven us to our vocation. Regardless of where one works, we all began as newly minted nurses, those with a vision of a future that would change lives for the better. Throughout our respective journeys, we have all faced challenges, including surges in patient volume, increased acuity levels, personal protective equipment (PPE), and staff shortages, putting nurses and nursing at risk—these and more have contributed to today's workforce and workplace issues.

1

We're about to delve into today's workforce, the many avenues open to RNs, and how the stark reality of our work environments has transformed the once-idealized image of our profession.

Chapter 1

From Entry Level to Academia . . . a Journey through the Stages and Phases of the Workforce

Enoh Ukpong

I have been working in healthcare for the past forty-eight years. My career has spanned multiple settings, and I have encountered the impact of workforce at each stage of my career. After all I have seen, my simple definition of a functional healthcare workforce is this: an adequate number of qualified professionals effectively delivering care to the patients.

Transitions

As a Nigerian American, I came to the United States in January 1979 on a student visa to continue my nursing education. Prior to this, I had earned my nursing license (1975) and midwifery license (1976) in Nigeria. While in the US, I advanced from nursing assistant to licensed practical nurse (LPN) before finally obtaining my registered nurse (RN) license in Massachusetts. I was a full-time college student throughout this career trajectory. I earned my bachelor's and master's degrees from Anna Maria College, in Paxton, Massachusetts, and a doctoral degree from Columbia Pacific University in 1989.

My responsibilities involved adequate staffing and workforce. Those of you who have been in the profession for more than a few years have seen the change in care delivery models firsthand. Each sequential change was touted as an improvement over the previous one—or at least that was what we were told.

We transitioned from team nursing in the '70s and early '80s to primary nursing based on acuity levels. Patient acuity (severity of illness) impacts care delivery and staffing needs. Staffing guidelines vary from one setting to another. Periodic workforce confrontations and strikes evolve around staffing ratios and benefits. When staffing is inadequate, patient safety is jeopardized, and staff satisfaction is compromised.

Academia . . . a New Awareness

When I transitioned to nursing education at Becker College (2001–2021), I gained a unique perspective on the workforce. Our curriculum requires qualified educators in multiple specialties. Recruiting and keeping those nursing specialists is easier said than done. All healthcare settings require qualified staffing to meet the needs of those we serve in cities around the country and across the globe.

While we have always experienced cyclical shortages, awareness escalated because of the pandemic. Healthcare workers stepped up during and after the pandemic, the most critical and dangerous period in recent years. They endured emotional and physical stress, dramatic infection-control protocols, increased patient volume, and unsurpassed acuity levels and deaths. It was a very tough period for the healthcare industry, and those on the frontlines were frustrated, overwhelmed, and overworked. Younger members of the healthcare team opted out.

They pursued careers that were less demanding of their physical and emotional health. Older members of the healthcare team chose retirement. Schools and colleges closed or went online. Virtual care was delivered through telehealth. Mental health disorders were prolific. Our system was in crisis.

The crisis seemed insurmountable, but it could be resolved with a commitment to the development of an engaged workforce—a workforce with a passion for the profession and an understanding of the need to grow our respective teams, in practice and education.

Nurse Leader Role

What can a nurse leader, in practice or education, do? As nurse leaders, we must value existing staff and create a culturally safe environment that attracts new team members. Partnering with educational institutions offers a pipeline to possible recruits. Post-graduate programs support continuous learning and career acceleration. The nursing profession is still attractive, thanks to the possibilities of delivering care and education in diverse settings. As a nursing professor, I have personally helped to enrich the workforce by creating cadres of future and current nurses. As a foreign-trained nurse, I took advantage of the opportunity to enhance my career, expand my horizons, and envision my future. With a terminal degree, I have worked with students who, like me, see nursing as a lifetime of opportunity. As a leader, you must listen with intention to your employees, be supportive and available when they need you, and actively encourage their professional growth. With these steps in place, you can create and sustain a healthy workforce for our collective future.

A healthy workforce is engaged in the mission and vision of the organization and the profession. While delivery models have changed and will continue to change, we cannot be replaced by drones and technology.

We can advocate for nurses and nursing by listening to the issues employees are facing. We can start to think differently, track progress, and share our results. We can support research into workforce-related issues, and we can support our teams by providing them with what they need to deliver quality, effective care. This will result in a happier, more productive nurse, one who is empowered to deliver on the promise of service excellence. At the same time, this will result in a grateful and satisfied patient. It all begins with a psychologically and physically safe environment—a healthy work environment. We owe this to our employees and to those for whom we care.

Reflection

I often think about my own career, and how I might view the situation and circumstances if I were starting over. What would I tell a younger version of myself?

I would tell a young version of myself to "GO FOR IT!" It's worth all the sacrifice and hard work. You will only go through this once in your lifetime. Once you earn your RN license, there are so many opportunities and career paths available to you. You will never think of switching to any other profession, because there is none like nursing—there is none like healthcare.

Chapter 2

Advanced Practice Nursing . . . Advancing Healthcare in America

Brent Dunworth

R enowned for problem-solving abilities, a commitment to education, and solution-oriented innovation, nurses have historically stepped in to address care deficiencies, leading to the growth of advanced practice nursing (APN) specialties. Recognizing unmet population care needs and creating avenues to address are the hallmarks of APN roles.

Nurse anesthetists, known in the United States as certified registered nurse anesthetists (CRNAs), have played a crucial role in anesthesia care for well over a century. Beginning in the nineteenth century, during the Civil War, nurse anesthetists made an indelible mark on our healthcare landscape. In 1909, Sister Mary Bernard became the first nurse to specialize in hospital-based anesthesia. Consistent with advances in practice, the role of CRNAs expanded, leading to the creation of a specialty nursing society, the American Association of Nurse Anesthetists (AANA). The AANA has been instrumental in setting professional standards and advocating for CRNAs. Today,

CRNAs are licensed to practice in all fifty states and are the sole anesthesia providers in many rural hospitals.[1]

The mid-twentieth century brought a growing need for primary care services, especially in underserved areas. To meet that need, the role of the nurse practitioner (NP) appeared. We credit Drs. Loretta Ford, a public health nurse, and Henry Silver, a physician, with the establishment of the first NP program at the University of Colorado in 1965. They hoped to expand the public-health and preventive-care components of nursing by incorporating certain aspects of the medical model. The NP role continues to expand, with practitioners gaining the authority to diagnose, treat, and prescribe medications, which has been crucial in addressing healthcare shortages. Today's NPs play a vital role across specialties and settings. Their contributions have been endorsed by organizations like the American Association of Nurse Practitioners (AANP), which advocates for the role and rights of NPs.[2]

Nurse-midwifery in the US began in the early twentieth century, influenced by the British midwife system and the public health movement. The Maternity Center Association (MCA) in New York City established the first nurse-midwifery education program. By integrating nursing care with midwifery skills, nurse-midwives were able to meet the needs of underserved, rural, and urban populations. By the 1950s, nurse-midwives were primary care providers for childbirth, especially for low-risk pregnancies. The American College of Nurse-Midwives (ACNM) sets professional standards, accredits midwifery education programs, and advocates for nurse-midwives. Today, certified nurse-midwives (CNMs) are licensed to practice in all fifty states, providing comprehensive women's healthcare from adolescence to postmenopause.[3]

Clinical nurse specialists (CNSs) have a storied history that can be traced back to the 1950s. With a pressing need for specialized nurses to provide expert care, CNSs emerged, leading initiatives for improved patient outcomes, and spearheading research endeavors. Rutgers University was home to the first CNS program in 1954. Combining clinical expertise in disease/pathophysiology with a focus on nursing care, the CNSs oversaw education, consultation, and research. The 1970s saw the growth of CNS programs nationally, with the formal recognition of CNSs by the American Nurses Association (ANA) in 1974. Currently, we see CNSs contribute evidence-based practices, quality improvement, and the enhancement of patient care across diverse settings.[4]

The COVID-19 Pandemic . . . a Call for Advanced Practice Nursing

The insidious spread of COVID-19 shook the core of the global healthcare system in 2019. As nations grappled with overflowing hospitals, dwindling medical resources, and an overstretched healthcare workforce, the necessity for nimble and adaptive solutions became painfully clear. A positive aspect to this daunting crisis was the flexibility, ingenuity, and consolidation of the role of APNs, who have become central figures in pandemic response across healthcare settings.

Regulatory Reforms: Bridging the Care Gap

Autonomous practice has always been a concern in the medical community; many regions have imposed restrictions on APNs to limit their ability to practice without oversight. The pressing exigencies of the pandemic forced a reevaluation. In the US, numerous states either suspended or amended their scope-of-practice regulations, granting APNs the ability to operate without mandatory physician supervision.[5] By enabling APNs to harness their full training and capabilities, these changes enhanced the agility of healthcare response, making services more accessible to patients in dire times.

Hospital Privileging: Elevating the Role of APNs

The pandemic placed overwhelming pressure on hospitals worldwide. In response, many expanded the "privileging" rights of APNs. APNs were entrusted with triaging, admitting, managing, and discharging patients, resulting in improved flow and comprehensive care even during peaks of the crisis. Advanced triage and critical care skills were leveraged like never before to manage the overwhelming volume of hospitalized patients who were experiencing rapid cardiopulmonary decompensation.[6]

Telehealth: The New Frontier

The pandemic catalyzed a telehealth revolution. With in-person visits becoming challenging, virtual consultations became the norm. APNs, with their multifaceted training, seamlessly integrated into this new mode of care delivery. Their ability to assess, diagnose, and even prescribe remotely was instrumental in ensuring that people received timely care, even from the safety of their homes.[7] APN care eased patient management through remote monitoring technology. Those who began to decompensate were directed to the hospital for admission. On the post-discharge side, APNs provided similar follow-up to ensure convalescence.

Addressing the Primary Care Deficit

Even before the pandemic, a glaring dearth of primary care providers was clear, particularly in regions where physicians were scarce or overwhelmed.[8] The pandemic heightened this need. APNs, equipped with advanced education and a patient-centric approach, emerged as pivotal figures, ensuring both COVID-19 care and chronic disease management.

Introduction and Expansion of Specialized Roles

The unique demands of the pandemic necessitated specialized roles. APNs found themselves wearing multiple hats, from contact tracers to infection preventionists, and even tele-ICU monitors. Their broad clinical experience and adaptability meant they could be quickly trained and deployed in these specialized roles, further amplifying their importance in the healthcare chain.[9]

Embracing Holistic Care: The APN Advantage

Beyond the immediate and clear physical toll, the pandemic also escalated mental health challenges. Lockdowns, isolation, and general uncertainty heightened anxiety and stress. APNs, trained in a holistic model of care that emphasizes the mind-body connection, were uniquely positioned to address this dual challenge. Their approach ensured that patients received comprehensive care, addressing both their physical ailments and psychosocial distress.[10]

Education and Training Reinforcements

Cognizant of the growing role of APNs during the pandemic, institutions began to assimilate pandemic preparedness and telehealth training into their curricula, equipping future APNs with the ability to manage similar challenges.[11]

A Global Event Showcases Advanced Practice Nursing Versatility

The pandemic illuminated APNs' critical role, flexibility, adaptability, and comprehensive care approach. Regulatory, operational, and educational shifts underscored our importance and set the stage for a unified and resilient healthcare system in the future.

Reflection

Progress in nursing education tailored to address US demands has consistently yielded exceptional outcomes. Nurses' inherent ability to employ unique critical-thinking skills has facilitated tangible and significant enhancements nationwide. While the challenges of refining US healthcare delivery might seem overwhelming, nurses consistently step up, as evidenced during the pandemic. Nurses will persist in their pursuit of excellence, even as they navigate emerging innovations in health promotion. Evidence consistently supports advanced practice delivery models as safe, adding value to access and patient satisfaction.[12]

Our healthcare system treads a delicate balance, with nurses shouldering immense physical and emotional strains. Ensuring the resilience of nurses requires a concerted effort and an ongoing assessment of their workloads. Overcoming this challenge can make the nursing profession even more attractive, gauged by nurses' ability to maintain rigorous performance standards. Falling below this gold standard often correlates with feelings of dissatisfaction and burnout, potentially curtailing a nurse's active career span in the field.[13] For years, APNs have advanced healthcare delivery within the US. They are now setting the standard and raising the bar for collaborative workforces that work.

Chapter 3

A Global Perspective

Benjamin Joel Breboneria

The Joy in the Journey . . . This Is Nursing!

Right now, as I think of my nursing career, I realize how blessed I am—for the journey, the experiences, and the people who have had an impact on my life and helped me to find my purpose.

The Challenge

My early career was replete with feelings of failure, precipitated by a lack of experience with people and an inability to deal with my own emotions, find my power, and realize my vision. As a young professional, I struggled with career, life, and material possessions. At the same time, I was in discovery mode and trying to find myself.

Early in our careers, we are blessed to meet many colleagues and forge new relationships—but we could also be yearning for belonging. In retrospect, it was this longing that could make or break me. It was the impulsivity that often took me off the path and in a direction that was not right for me. I learned to take risks, find meaning, and build on my childhood experiences, some of which were painful, to find meaning. I sought new experiences, and I left the comfort and familiarity of the Philippines for the unknown. I decided to meet diverse kinds of people, try new things, and engage in relationships for better or for worse. In short, my impulsivity as a young nurse wanting to feel that sense of belonging always drove me.

Coming to a country that was never part of my plans (and that was once a place I never thought could become an avenue for my growth) opened my mind and my heart. When I arrived in Saudi Arabia, I had no experience with diverse cultures, and I had an extensive learning curve ahead of me. From communication, dialect, core values, and local customs, I gained an appreciation for my peers and a deeper understanding of authentic connections and openness. I entered a workspace and workplace in which there was an opportunity to learn about our differences as human beings, making each of us more grounded and accepting. As I have continued to grow in this space, I have expanded my reach as a nurse leader and educator. My intentionality for growth and advancement helped me find ways to add value and purpose to those I serve.

Lifelong Learning and a Purpose for Being

Throughout my career, I never ceased to continue learning—taking courses, being mentored by the best of the best people in the nursing profession, and learning about who I am and my own learning needs. Through that discipline, I soon realized that I am fond of listening to the stories of nurses in practice. Gaining knowledge and new skills became a comfort zone that was always within my reach. But what led me to stories was their unique formula: distinctive, lived experiences that resonate with emotions common to all people striving to find purpose in this lifetime.

An Attitude of Gratitude

Working in another country led me to discover my leadership and my passion toward others. These lived experiences organically transformed me with the realization that what makes me happy is being kind to the people around me, being who I am to the external world, understanding that life is a series of up-and-down moments, and embracing that all these elements are critical to a journey of gratitude.

One of the most unforgettable experiences I had was when one of the service cleaners at our facility approached me, held my hand, put it to his chest, and told me words that I will never forget. He said, "Your heart is big." It was a human moment and a deep connection that made me emotional, connecting me to the values instilled in me by my parents as a young child. Their teachings made me who I am today. That statement by a Bangladeshi colleague with limited English, one who worked hard and struggled to support a family, was overwhelming. They may have lacked belongings, but they expressed gratitude for the small things they did have. This random act of human kindness strongly affirmed to me that touching other people's lives knows no boundaries; race, language, and appearance do not matter. My ability to be my authentic self opened a door to communication. Knowing that I made a difference in the life of someone else inspired me to continually strive to do the same for our profession.

Leveraging Our Authenticity

I believe that we have a unique opportunity to leverage ourselves as brands within our specialty practice or education. In school, we learned to promote a positive image of nurses and nursing, but we may forget that every individual nurse can contribute to that goal. Every nurse has the potential to share experiences, values, feelings, emotions, and stories that have enriched their lives.

Contemporary nursing education affords us the chance to explore media training, personal branding, networking, executive presence, and other human or soft skills that support our growth as professionals and as people. We can leverage learning and experience and grow the profession.

The Pandemic Effect

We saw how the global pandemic affected not just how we live our lives but also how it changed healthcare. These kinds of uncertainties gave us a realization that life is short; it is important to live our lives in the present moment and try our best to create an impact on whatever brings us joy. The pandemic showed the true value of nurses in times of uncertainty and crisis. For that reason, among others, the current staffing shortages are a key concern.

Change Is a Constant

How nurses and nursing are viewed can reflect negatively on the profession. The healthcare environment is sometimes uncivil and unpleasant. Stress is ongoing and leads to burnout. We know that we can benefit from the opportunity to change and bring positivity to the workforce and workplace.

Although often overlooked, gratitude allows us to express our appreciation to nurses, our modern-day unsung heroes who put their lives at risk to save more lives and ensure those lives will continue. Demonstrating gratitude, generosity, and concern for others strengthens our self-awareness. Deep gratitude for small acts of kindness can encourage us, change us, enable us to persevere through hardships, build our resilience, and, most importantly, inspire us to pay it forward and continue to help others.

Each nurse's strength comes from their ability to overcome problems and adversity. As Sharon Cox[1] shared, "Expressing gratitude builds a bridge to other people and invites them to cross it." Beyond merely a bridge, expressed gratitude embodies the passing of the baton, an impetus that propels an individual to pay it forward, and a contagious desire to pour oneself into the service of others. Fostering the importance of expressing gratitude is essential. Even in this small act, we encourage nurses to develop a stronger sense of confidence in their own skills and their ability to help others and continue their dedication to the profession.

Reflection

In retrospect, I would tell a younger version of myself about the joy in my personal and professional journey. That younger version of myself, the one that carried the trauma of the past internally, who was driven by dark circumstances, has chosen a profession of pride, joy, and accomplishment. This is a lifelong journey with a focus on grit, authenticity, kindness, gratitude, and joy—for the privilege of influencing the lives of others. This allows me to clearly see the hero that lies within each of us!

Chapter 4

Normalizing Bias Training

Nikki Akparewa

Our Greatest Challenge

The greatest challenge facing the nursing profession today is our inability to embrace how systemic acceptance of incivility is affecting our workforce as well as the patients that we have sworn to uphold and protect. Incivility is behavior that is rude, demeaning, or demoralizing to another. I believe challenges like persistent systemic incivilities (such as lateral violence, hierarchical silos, and especially the myth of martyrdom) ultimately devalue our profession and drain our emotional and social capital. As a health equity coach for the past decade, my work has focused on protecting, valuing, and holding in the light of persons whose voices have been historically marginalized. These voices are on the very periphery of our concern. Indeed, we have grappled with nursing shortages since the mid-twentieth century. The fact that not much has changed points to the nature of structural barriers, including incivility among and against nurses. Nurses can heal and restore; they can remedy not only physical maladies but social and emotional ills as well.

Why Nurses

Nurses are equipped to promote restorative justice, and yet we are so mired in a culture of white supremacy that we ignore the wide-open world of critical consciousness. White supremacy culture demands an orientation to whiteness to the exclusion of everything else. This minimizes and ignores the contributions, beliefs, norms, and values of other groups. This systemic incivility has led to worsened outcomes for minoritized patients because nurses of color are underrepresented and are not presented with the same promotional opportunities as their white counterparts. When will we admit that these endemic challenges are hurting our profession and our patients?

Pandemic: Impact on Healthcare

Prior to the pandemic, it was difficult to get the attention of academic and clinical nurse leaders. Like a true public health nurse's clarion call, I have long expressed the urgency of acting against incivility to retain our nursing talent. What I see now is that healthcare leaders are addressing low-hanging fruit, such as in-house implicit bias training, but the long game has yet to be actualized. The long game is diverse representation from the C-suite to the bedside; it is transparency and accountability in diversity, equity, and inclusion (DEI) practices tied to the bottom line; it is the aggressive retention of nurses of color.

Both the pandemic and the national moral reckoning with police brutality on African American persons, most notably in the aftermath of George Floyd's murder, brought nursing to her knees as we struggled with many realities at once. We experienced moral distress with mandatory requirements to work longer hours and the risk of exposure to illness. Nurses of color faced a dual pandemic: the experience of workplace racism and COVID-19 synergized to their detriment. In my workbook *The Clinician's Guide to Microaggressions & Unconscious Bias*,[1] I explore how we can begin the steep climb toward reckoning with racism in nursing and furnish practical tools for any nurse who is willing to do the work.

Since the pandemic, I have found that more nurse leaders are ready to listen. There has been a rush to put policies in place that address health equity both in academic and clinical practice. The National Commission to Address Racism in Nursing, formed by the American Nurses Association (ANA) in 2021, found ways to deepen conversations about ways that the ANA has been silent or complicit in the incivility toward nurses of color. Other national healthcare leaders acted quickly, rising to the challenge of addressing these structural barriers that have amounted to generational curses. I've had academic and clinical partners approach me asking, "How do we address these structural and systemic barriers in nursing, both on the unit and in education?" As the keynote speaker at nursing conferences, I've stressed the importance of a multimodal public health approach to addressing our most recalcitrant challenges. What I have learned is that there is a will, by many, to begin the work of acknowledging historical harms, and to understand the strategy for restorative practices. This is opening the doors for forgiveness and ultimately mutual prosperity and a minimization of suffering.

Nursing's Role in Recruitment, Retention, and a Healthy Workforce

In June of 2023, the US Supreme Court struck down race-based affirmative action in higher education, placing increased scrutiny on DEI practices that would promote civility.[2] We must not become complacent in addressing structural problems, including those that impact drivers of equitable recruitment and retention of a healthy workforce—like understanding the impact that race has on quality of life. I believe that the nursing profession can ensure a healthy workforce. We embody the principles of compassion. Pioneers of our profession such as Lillian Wald, Mary Eliza Mahoney, and Ernest Grant have risked their colleagues' disapproval, their reputation, and sometimes their livelihood so that they might help create a world in which social injustices would not be the narrative that determined a person's life expectancy or quality. The stakes are much higher now, for now we cannot feign ignorance of the harms of our sociocultural leanings. We now live in a world where the income gap is ever widening, patients are sicker, and only 15 percent of nurses say they will continue in the job in a year. We must not watch; we must act.

Now is the time to restore dignity not only to our noble profession but also to our patients, who feel the sting of less compassionate care. Doing better begins with acknowledging human dignity. It begins with seeing our patients as creative, resourceful, and whole—and not being comfortable with seeing them as "frequent flyers" or persons who are "non-adherent" to our instructions. We must create the world we want to see, starting with our systems. Nursing institutions need to seek diverse representation of nurses of color across professional trajectories, including diverse faculty members in our nursing schools.

Our Future

The future could be bright—but it could just as easily dim. We have difficult choices to make. We are growing our workforce; many nursing schools are accepting more nurses into the profession . . . but are we retaining them? We won't retain nurses if we don't provide the flexibility, transparency, and trust they've earned. This means creating safe environments, maintaining safe staffing ratios, and ensuring that we are recruiting nurses from all socioeconomic backgrounds, experiences, ages, and identities. We can advocate for nurses in the health-care environment by being conscious of the truth that nursing is both an art and a science. This means that our rigid criteria and pass/fail mentality do not serve our nurses or the profession. We must engage as mentors and coaches, allowing for error, allowing for redirection, promoting clear feedback, and becoming allies to one another. This work will come with the hard truth that we've missed the mark; sincere apologies will have to be made, followed by swift action. I speak with such hope, confidence, and resilience because I sincerely believe in the right to repair. We can repair the damage that has plagued our profession for generations. I believe that we are better together; our complexity allows us to resolve tremendous challenges. With an inclusive approach, we can generate more complex and sustainable solutions.

Reflection

I would tell a younger version of myself to "mind the gaps." As a nursing student and novice nurse, I was unprepared for the rigor of practice. While I completed my requirements, that was just the beginning. I was a frightened young woman who had moved alone from Seattle to Baltimore to start my career. Had I not had preceptors who were patient and kind (to outshine those who weren't), had I not had mentors who saw my potential and pushed me toward greater heights, had I stopped believing in myself when the naysayers were trying to tear me down, I would have given up. There were gaps that I didn't anticipate, and I thought that I wasn't given enough preparation. Looking back, I see that it was all for my own growth. Had I not had to jump those hoops to get to my next achievement, I wouldn't have the strength of my conviction or passion today. Sure, I have some scars too; nurses hurting each other cuts deeply, especially when it feels unwarranted. However, these scars make my story what it is now. And finally, I'm grateful.

Chapter 5

Championing Creativity

Byron Carlisle

The Challenge

The greatest challenge facing our professional workforce today is creating a healthy work environment in which nurses care for patients. A significant characteristic of a healthy work environment is appropriate staffing.[1] Nurse staffing is a multifaceted issue, and it is extremely difficult to objectively advocate for change. Different members of the healthcare team have different concepts of nurse staffing. To some, proper staffing means staying within a budgeted, fixed nurse-to-patient ratio, or accurately scoring a patient's acuity, or maximizing an employee's responsibilities to their full potential within their scope of practice. Each factor influences staffing decisions.

Nurses enter the healthcare profession because they want to help someone in need and make a positive impact on patients' lives, but it is incredibly challenging to consistently capture accurate data that allows for nursing representatives to objectively advocate for additional help. As a unit manager, trying to keep talent and decreasing the unit's turnover rate is one of the many challenges I've faced. When the unit's staff is consistent and professionals stay, continuity of care can be established.[2] Once this baseline is set up, we must ask these questions: 1) Do we have the right number of nurses to care for our patients? 2) How do we know? 3) How do we find out?

The Pandemic Effect

In 2017, I was fortunate to manage a neuroscience intensive care unit (NSICU) that changed its nurse-to-patient (RN:PT) ratio from 1 registered nurse (RN) for every 1.75 patients (1:1.75) to 1 RN for every 1.5 (1:1.5) patients. This change in ratio allowed the department to add 4.3 full-time equivalents (FTEs) to the unit's workforce. This was an amazing win for the patients, the unit, and the hospital, but we still needed to fill the FTEs, keep the staff, and then measure the outcome. We creatively used added staff, recovering patients directly from the operating room in a 1:1 fashion for the first hour post-op based on the guidelines of the American Society of PeriAnesthesia Nurses (ASPAN). With this change, we saw a decrease in falls and an increase in staff retention. Our turnover rate dropped from 19.8 percent in 2017, to 16.7 percent in 2018, and 5.7 percent in 2019.[3] As we entered the pandemic, our staff retention set us up to positively affect our continuity of care and allowed time for leadership to devote to coaching and developing the bedside staff.

During the pandemic, our hospital experienced an increase in staff attrition, and our five adult intensive care units became more reliant on partnerships than we ever had before, as we had to use a central staffing office.[4] RNs were scheduled in their home units, but our central staffing office would consider all ICUs' patient acuity levels and deploy RNs to units most in need. Increasing COVID-19 patient acuity due to multiple complications, plus hospital attrition, began to have a bigger impact on staffing ratios.

Average RN:PT ratios in the NSICU are shown in Table 1.

AVERAGE RN: PT RATIOS IN THE NSICU
2019 dayshift (1:1.67), nightshift (1:1.61)
2020 dayshift (1:1.69), nightshift (1:1.64)
2021 dayshift (1:1.84), nightshift (1:1.87)
2022 dayshift (1:1.88), nightshift (1:1.86)

Table 1

One can see that there is more to it than ratios—retention must be considered for achieving and maintaining appropriate staffing.

Overcoming Potential Barriers

In March of 2020, when the pandemic was declared, my unit's leadership team discussed what we knew about the pandemic, what the staff wanted to know, and how our leadership team could communicate essential information to staff. Since we float nursing staff to our medical intensive care unit (MICU), our leadership team took the initiative and partnered with our MICU. We learned about our infection prevention processes, and then trained our staff on caring for the COVID-19 patient population.[5]

During this time, I also attended an advisory board lecture titled "Leading through Crisis," presented by Carol Boston-Fleischhauer.[6] In her lecture, Boston-Fleischhauer covered topics such as nursing shortages, increasing burnout, and early COVID-19 pandemic data. But one of the most beneficial takeaways for me as a leader was her slide titled "Psychological and Logistical Barriers That Promote Fear." This slide addressed what staff need to feel safe at work—staffing, equipment, and training—plus what staff need to feel safe going into work, like childcare, transportation, and the ability to protect their families.

We then listened to multiple weekly updates offered by our president, chief executive officer, and chief nurse executive. Their input supplied context for our biweekly staff presentation. Virtual presentations added value; we could record these updates and send them to staff who were unable to attend the live meeting. Communicating with transparency allowed us to connect with staff twice a week, encouraging open questions and dialogue. This process helped us lead our staff into the unknown with as much knowledge as possible. Change was constant, and it was challenging to keep up with it all. Our open forum allowed our staff to share their experiences when floated to various intensive care units (ICUs). Open lines of communication and preventing as many surprises as possible helped us to create and maintain a healthy work environment and to keep staff.

Engagement and Advocacy

Everyone is busy. For us to advocate for the nursing workforce, we need to continue to explore how nursing units can objectively capture and report being overstaffed, appropriately staffed, or understaffed. Variables such as number of staff, number of patients, patients' acuity, patient outcomes, patient satisfaction, staff satisfaction, and fiscal impact should be measured and evaluated. We then need to be transparent about our findings and publish the outcomes to keep the conversation ongoing. Thinking outside the box to advocate for added help will be necessary to make sure nurses are getting the help they need.

Reflection

You have the power to contribute to a sound, healthy work environment, one that attracts and retains staff and delivers good outcomes, but your role is to first take care of yourself, at work and at home. Ensure that you take your lunch and biological breaks. Identify a hobby that brings you joy and in which you can take part when you are away from work. Be grateful for your peers and for your ability to make a difference in the lives of others. Champion creative ways to manage your life and your profession.

Chapter 6

Navigating the Challenges and Opportunities in Modern Nursing

Bob Dent

The Challenge

As we enter a new era in healthcare, nursing faces an unprecedented challenge: the relentless demand for skilled nursing care amid shifting demographics, an aging population, and increasing healthcare complexity. This challenge demands immediate attention and innovative solutions. Demographic shifts, particularly in the nursing profession and patient population, pose a critical concern. The nursing workforce is aging, with a staggering one million nurses expected to retire by 2030. This impending exodus of experienced nurses creates a severe shortage of seasoned professionals just as the demand for healthcare services escalates due to an aging population. The baby boomer generation's transition into their golden years has resulted in a substantial increase in elderly individuals requiring complex care. This places an overwhelming burden on nurses, who must now supply specialized care to a progressively frail and vulnerable population.

Advancements in medical science and technology have led to increasingly intricate treatments, therapies, and interventions. While these innovations hold promise for improved patient outcomes, they also mandate the need for updating one's knowledge and skills. This ongoing challenge demands that nurses not only keep pace with these changes, but also that they adapt to innovative technologies and workflows.

In the face of these challenges, staffing shortages have worsened, leading to burnout among nurses. Insufficient staffing levels were linked to poor patient outcomes prior to the pandemic. Some hospitals have opted to cut nursing hours as a cost-saving measure, which not only jeopardizes patient safety but also contributes to nurses leaving the profession prematurely due to the immense strain on their physical and mental well-being. Addressing today's unparalleled issues will require innovative solutions and a concerted effort to ensure that nursing remains a vibrant and sustainable profession capable of delivering high-quality care to a diverse and aging population.

Changes Impacting Healthcare

Significant shifts in nurse staffing, including increased reliance on temporary staff, travel nurses, and agency personnel, have had a profound impact on healthcare delivery. While these shifts supplied short-term fixes, they also brought adverse consequences, including reduced continuity of care, lowered morale among permanent staff, and elevated costs for facilities.

Linda Aiken,[1] a global advocate for safe nurse-to-patient staffing ratios, has addressed the significance of nurse-patient ratios as a measure of staffing adequacy. Responses have varied. Some states introduced legislation mandating specific nurse-patient ratios or safe staffing policies, with the aim of ensuring patient safety and care quality. However, this posed challenges for some facilities due to variations in patient needs, acuity, and the availability of qualified nursing staff. Not every patient is the same, and not every nurse is the same in terms of skill, knowledge, and experience.

Technological advancements in healthcare, such as electronic health records (EHRs) and workforce management software, promised more efficient staffing solutions. These tools improved data collection and scheduling processes but also required nurses to adapt to new systems. This transition sometimes resulted in initial disruptions to workflow. Changes in staffing strategies highlighted the healthcare industry's efforts to address staffing challenges and optimize patient care, but temporary fixes were not a panacea, and technology required adaptation and training.

As healthcare evolves, striking the right balance between staffing flexibility, patient safety, and technological integration is still a critical challenge for nurse leaders and healthcare administrators. These pre-pandemic developments laid the groundwork for addressing staffing issues, which became even more critical during the pandemic's unprecedented demands on healthcare systems.

Our Collective Future

To secure a robust and healthy nursing workforce for the future, we must adopt a comprehensive approach to both recruitment and retention strategies, as seen on the next page.

Recruitment Strategies

- **Early Exposure:** Encouraging early exposure to the nursing profession through school programs, internships, and mentorship opportunities is vital. This can lay the foundation for future nursing careers.
- **Diversity and Inclusion:** Prioritizing diversity and inclusion better mirrors the patient population, fostering cultural competency in care delivery.
- **Streamlined Education:** We must make education more accessible and affordable. Accelerated programs, online courses, and financial assistance can attract a broader spectrum of aspiring nurses.

Retention Strategies

- **Mentorship and Support:** By pairing experienced nurses with newcomers, we supply emotional support, guidance, and a sense of belonging, effectively mitigating burnout, and bolstering retention.
- **Work-Life Balance:** Promoting flexible scheduling, part-time work opportunities, and a comprehensive benefits package is essential. Ensuring that nurses can maintain fulfilling personal lives alongside their demanding careers is crucial to retaining their dedication.
- **Professional Development:** An investment in professional development is an investment in skills, advanced education, and updates in healthcare practices.
- **Recognition and Well-Being:** Recognizing and celebrating the hard work of nurses is vital and requires a workplace culture that places nurse well-being at the forefront, offers mental health resources, and encourages self-care.

Our Future . . . Advocacy

Advocacy plays a significant role in ensuring the well-being of nurses and fostering healthcare environments conducive to delivering quality care:

- Policy Advocacy: Nurses must actively engage in advocacy efforts aimed at influencing policy changes at the local, state, and national levels. This advocacy encompasses pressing for optimal nurse-patient ratios and staffing standards, safe working conditions, and equitable compensation.

- Professional Organizations: Active participation in professional nursing organizations is paramount. These organizations serve as platforms for collective advocacy, enabling the dissemination of best practices and the amplification of nurses' voices.

- Educational Advocacy: Nurses should advocate for elevating nursing education standards and curricula that adequately prepare nurses for evolving healthcare needs. Additionally, advocating for increased funding for nursing education programs ensures a steady supply of well-prepared nursing professionals.

- Patient Advocacy: At the heart of nursing practice is patient advocacy. Nurses must remain steadfast in their commitment to ensuring patients receive the highest quality care. This involves speaking up when safety concerns arise and advocating relentlessly for the best possible patient outcomes.

- Workplace Culture Advocacy: Nurses have a vital role in promoting workplace cultures characterized by respect, collaboration, and support. Advocating for policies and practices that prioritize nurse well-being, reduce burnout, and enhance job satisfaction is essential to sustaining a motivated and resolute nursing workforce.

Through active participation in these advocacy efforts, nurses not only safeguard their own professional interests but also contribute significantly to the betterment of the healthcare system. Advocacy empowers nurses to drive meaningful change, ultimately resulting in improved patient care and more supportive healthcare environments.

Reflections

Reflecting on my own nursing professional journey, if I could impart wisdom to my younger self embarking on a nursing career, it would encompass the following counsel:

- Passion and Purpose: Always hold close the understanding that nursing is a profession intricately woven with passion and purpose. Your actions as a nurse will directly shape the destinies of individuals and communities. Approach each day armed with empathy, kindness, and an unwavering dedication to effecting positive change.
- Lifelong Learning: Embrace the ethos of perpetual learning. The healthcare landscape is in a never-ending state of evolution. Therefore, staying abreast of the latest research, technology, and practices is indispensable for delivering the highest quality care possible.
- Resilience: Grasp the importance of cultivating resilience. Nursing can impose emotional and physical demands that require fortitude to navigate. Never hesitate to seek support from your peers, mentors, and

available mental health resources when faced with challenges and setbacks.

- Advocacy: Recognize the power of advocacy, not only on behalf of your patients but also for your own well-being and that of your colleagues. Advocate ardently for safe staffing levels, fair treatment, and a workplace culture that treasures and bolsters the nursing profession.
- Self-Care: Prioritize self-care as an irreplaceable aspect of your journey. The care you provide to others begins with caring for yourself. Carve out moments for respite, nurture your mental and physical health, and strive for equilibrium between your personal and professional life.
- Collaboration: Understand that nursing thrives on collaboration. Work harmoniously within interdisciplinary teams to deliver holistic care. Your colleagues, ranging from physicians to therapists, are invaluable reservoirs of knowledge and support, essential for achieving the best possible patient outcomes.

These serve as a compass guiding not only your nursing path but also your personal growth, ensuring a fulfilling and impactful journey in the world of healthcare.

Chapter 7

Creating a Culture of Emotional Safety in Healthcare

Joe Tye

A pervasive sense of dread permeates our society. Gallup's 2022 annual report tracking the world's emotional state concluded, "In 2021, negative emotions—the aggregate of the stress, sadness, anger, worry and physical pain that people feel every day—reached a new record in the history of Gallup's tracking."[1] Over the past decade—and especially since the pandemic—rudeness, incivility, bullying, and even violence have become normalized in our society. The impact has been especially severe in healthcare. Caregivers who were hailed as heroes during the early days of the pandemic now must worry about being verbally abused or physically assaulted. To protect the physical safety of staff, hospitals now routinely post warnings that assaulting a hospital staff member is a criminal act that will be prosecuted, something that would have been unthinkable ten years ago.

In Gallup's 2023 book, *Culture Shock*, authors Jim Clifton and Jim Harter state that teams where people believe their organization cares about their well-being "have higher customer engagement, profitability and productivity; lower turnover; and fewer safety incidents." They share Gallup's finding that employees who strongly agree their employer cares about their overall well-being are significantly more likely to be engaged in their work, less likely to experience burnout or be looking for another job, more likely to recommend their organization as a great place to work, and more likely to be thriving in their overall lives.[2]

Unfortunately, the authors also report that only about one in four US workers believe their organization's leaders really do care about their well-being.[3] Surveys that I conducted for members of the Association of California Nurse Leaders (ACNL) and for participants in the 2022 National Evidence-Based Practice Conference included the question, "Do you think your staff believes the organization is doing enough for their mental and emotional well-being?" Nearly half of responding nurse leaders responded, "Not at all," and fewer than 10 percent responded, "Absolutely yes." And these responses are from leaders![4] Frontline staff have an even dimmer perception. In a 2020 national survey of 1,425 frontline nurses by Trusted Health, 95 percent of respondents said that the healthcare industry does not prioritize or provide adequate resources for their mental and emotional well-being. The report concludes: "What we found is a profession in crisis. Not only are nurses reporting significant declines in their mental health; high levels of depression, stress and PTSD; moral injuries, and bouts of compassion fatigue, but nearly half of the respondents in our survey reported feeling less committed to the profession than they were before the pandemic."[5]

Emotional Safety and Psychological Safety

In his classic study, *On the Psychology of Military Incompetence*, Norman Dixon concluded that the primary difference between competent and incompetent military commanders is their ability, or inability, to manage their own anxiety. Those who don't are more likely to panic or become paralyzed.[6] High anxiety creates dysfunctional organizations. A core benefit of a culture of emotional safety is that it lowers anxiety levels and minimizes counterproductive attitudes and behaviors. Healthcare organizations should foster a culture that protects employee emotional safety to complement what they should already be doing to protect psychological safety—and to understand the difference.

Psychological safety is the keystone of just culture. It's the assurance that people can identify problems and errors, including their own, without fear of punishment, retribution, or humiliation. Its primary purpose is to eliminate patient safety incidents and encourage risk-taking innovation.

Emotional safety is the keystone of a culture of well-being. It's the assurance that leadership is committed to protecting the emotional health and well-being of staff from internal and external threats, and to assuring that help is available for emotional stress or trauma without shame or stigma.

Psychological safety is about the organization. Emotional safety is about the individual. These eight strategies will help leaders foster a stronger culture of emotional safety.

Strategy 1: Assess, Don't Assume

The higher one's position on the organizational chart, the rosier the glasses one tends to wear when making assumptions about the culture. The only way to truly have a pulse on your culture is to survey people—a lot. There are multiple proprietary tools available with validated survey questions and comparison groups to index your results against. SurveyMonkey and similar programs allow you to create your own questions. Survey fatigue is a fallacy; people love to be asked for their opinions about work; fatigue occurs when they don't think their responses will be acted upon.

Strategy 2: Practice Radical Transparency

Uncertainty is the greatest cause of anxiety. The best way to minimize uncertainty—and the rumor mill it fuels—is to communicate fully and often. With limited exceptions, leadership should share the same information (including financials) with frontline staff that they share with the board—as well as instruction on how to interpret that information and what it means for their work. Open-book management, popularized by Jack Stack and his team at Springfield ReManufacturing in what they called "the great game of business," is a great model for radical transparency.[7]

Strategy 3: Show Up

There has been an erosion of trust in leadership during the pandemic and its immediate aftermath, partly caused by the fact that in-person meetings were cancelled and many executives worked from home. Management by walking around, pioneered by Bill and Dave at Hewlett-Packard (now HP), and more recently popularized as the Gemba Walk, is an essential way for leaders to gauge the emotional climate of the workplace and to rebuild trust. Simply showing up without a script or an agenda and talking to people, listening to their concerns, and following up on promises made is one of the best ways to foster trust.

Strategy 4: Any Excuse for a Celebration

In preparation for my book *How the DAISY Foundation Has Influenced the Global Healthcare Landscape*, I conducted a survey of nurses and nurse leaders on my mailing list who had been honored with a DAISY Award. More than 90 percent of respondents said the award was one of the highlights of their career *and* that DAISY has had a positive impact on the culture of their organization.[8] To enhance a culture of emotional safety, leaders should take every opportunity to recognize people for their work and celebrate their accomplishments.

Strategy 5: Make Huddles Special with Rituals

Staff huddles should be a daily ritual in every unit and department, on every shift. Beyond the routine sharing of information, huddles should be a forum for sharing stories, recognition, and gratitude, and for fostering positive optimism.

Strategy 6: Intolerance for Toxic Emotional Negativity

Toxic emotional negativity—as reflected in chronic complaining, bullying, and rumormongering—is the emotional and spiritual equivalent of ambient cigarette smoke. It makes everyone sick. Emotional vampires suck the energy out of the room, suck the joy out of the work, and suck the life out of the victims by their emotional abuse. The Pickle Challenge for Charity, described at PicklePledge.com, creates a more positive environment by encouraging people to turn complaints into contributions. It's fun, it's free, and it can be life-changing for individuals and culturally transformative for organizations.

Strategy 7: Have a Clear Layoff Policy

In his book *Dying for a Paycheck*, Stanford business school professor Jeffrey Pfeffer shows how employee layoffs increase stress and anxiety, and often workload, among survivors while having minimal financial benefit to the organization.[9] To reduce anxiety and sustain emotional safety, organizations should create and communicate a clear policy about layoffs. That policy should emphasize that layoffs will be a last resort for cost-cutting, describe circumstances under which they might be implemented, and assure the best possible treatment for those impacted.

Strategy 8: Double Down on Culture

In response to the pandemic and subsequent financial challenges, many healthcare organizations have disinvested in culture by cutting out "discretionary" expenses such as travel to professional conferences, non-mandatory staff training, outside consultants, and leadership developments. The fractional impact these actions might have on financial performance could, over the long term, be more than outweighed by the deleterious impact on culture. Now is the time to increase, not reduce, your investments in culture.

Conclusion

With predictions that the healthcare staffing crisis will become increasingly dire in coming years, building a reputation for a culture of emotional safety is one of the most effective ways your organization can attract and retain the best talent.

Chapter 8

Innovation and the Healthcare Workforce

Tim Raderstorf

Healthcare innovation is at a critical juncture, moving from an often-overused buzzword to a vital force in the healthcare workforce. Innovation is the process of implementing new products, services, or solutions that create new value.[1] In today's healthcare landscape, the focus on value creation is paramount. From the introduction of value-based care through the Affordable Care Act of 2010 to the contemporary emphasis on maximizing profits and reducing costs among health system CEOs, innovation is the linchpin for the future of healthcare.

As innovation solidifies its presence in healthcare, its impact resonates throughout the healthcare workforce. At times, it has enhanced the lives of healthcare professionals, such as how Hoyer lifts and similar devices have reduced workplace injuries. However, it's arguable that innovation has occasionally hindered clinicians, particularly when dealing with electronic health records (EHRs). This dual nature prompts a fundamental question: Why should the healthcare workforce wholeheartedly embrace innovation?

In essence, the answer lies in the reality that there's no alternative. Healthcare innovation advances regardless of clinicians' involvement. To harness the potential for the workforce to influence innovation, active participation and partnership in the healthcare innovation journey are imperative. Success depends on our ability to unite and advocate for what's best for patients and ourselves as professionals. Not engaging in shaping future innovations means someone else will craft them for us, devoid of the healthcare perspective. Allowing those who understand the issues most intimately—namely, the healthcare workforce—to solve healthcare problems is essential for maximizing both impact and investment in healthcare innovation.

The Innovation Studio at The Ohio State University serves as a testament to the success of models that empower frontline healthcare workers to chart the future. This was achieved by setting up a maker space that empowers clinicians to address the most pressing challenges affecting them and their patients. The Innovation Studio equips teams with access to prototyping tools like 3D printers and laser cutters, facilitating the transformation of ideas into tangible solutions. These initiatives are further bolstered by mentorship and funding opportunities available through regular pitch events. By empowering frontline workers to take charge of problem-solving, the Innovation Studio epitomizes a model for clinicians to shape the trajectory of healthcare. Intriguingly, the benefits extend beyond the mere development of innovations that enhance outcomes. Engaging in the creative processes at the Innovation Studio has reportedly increased clinicians' likelihood of remaining with their current organization,[2] while generating new value for patients who benefit from these innovations. To explore this model further, visit TED.com and search for "The Participation Trophy Model for Innovation and Why It Works."

A Call for Collective Ambition within the Healthcare Workforce

The aftermath of the COVID-19 pandemic continues to inflict hardships on the healthcare workforce. Clinicians have been inundated with calls to fortify their professional resilience in response to the challenges within their organizations. Developing personal resilience, as outlined in the Well-Being section of this book, is a praiseworthy strategy for improving individual health, yet it also sustains underperforming and flawed systems. When organizations urge their employees to cultivate professional resilience, they are essentially asking them to adapt to system inadequacies. Such an approach implies that employees striving to rectify systemic issues would somehow not result in system improvements.

An alternative response to the call for professional resilience is to embrace the concept of collective ambition. In the realm of collective ambition, employees within an organization identify the aspects that require fixing. Instead of conforming to the system's status quo, they acknowledge the issues, assume ownership, and actively transform the system to eliminate the identified problems. No longer focused on changing themselves for the system, those who are collectively ambitious change the system for themselves!

The Healthcare Workforce and the Future of Innovation

Embracing healthcare innovation necessitates a consensus on two fundamental truths. First, it is imperative to enhance the healthcare system. Second, this pursuit of improvement will invariably disrupt the status quo. Accepting this reality can be challenging, as it often engenders short-term turbulence. Job losses, apprehension of obsolescence, and resistance to change are all plausible experiences for clinicians in an innovative environment. Thriving amid this disruption and reaping the long-term benefits of innovation mandates an understanding of the answers to four crucial questions:

How Will Innovation Improve the Healthcare Workforce?

Innovation continually pushes the boundaries between the known and the unknown,[3] offering immense potential to enhance the healthcare workforce. Progress is often the outcome when boundaries are tested. Recent advancements in healthcare, such as artificial intelligence (AI), telehealth, extended reality (XR), and wearable health devices, exemplify this progress.

Many of these technologies are on the path to becoming integral parts of the healthcare norm. Robotic-assisted surgery, once feared as a surgeon replacement, now enjoys widespread acceptance for its ability to enhance patient outcomes through heightened precision while relieving surgeons of undue strain. AI-powered diagnostic tools continue to advance, showcasing the capability to analyze medical data and images more swiftly and accurately than humans. Properly embraced, this technology empowers healthcare professionals to make more informed decisions.

Technologies like virtual reality (VR) and augmented reality (AR)—now collectively referred to as XR—offer immersive training experiences for healthcare students and professionals. These technologies function as modern simulation labs, enabling learners to practice complex procedures within a safe, controlled environment, thereby better preparing the healthcare workforce.

The greatest potential for enhancing the healthcare workforce lies in unleashing the collaborative capabilities of innovative tools. Cloud-based platforms and electronic health records (EHRs) facilitate the sharing of patient data, fostering greater coordination and personalized care. Although the journey toward improving the healthcare workforce through collaboration tools has encountered obstacles, its potential to benefit patients, advance knowledge, and enhance outcomes on a broader scale is vast.

How Will Innovation Inhibit the Healthcare Workforce?

Despite the transformative potential of progress and innovation in healthcare, they also pose certain challenges that can hinder the workforce. A poignant example is the EHR, a major twenty-first-century innovation in healthcare. Clinicians were promised that EHRs would revolutionize patient care, and few would dispute that notion. However, many clinicians argue that this transformation has negatively impacted healthcare overall, with nurses spending 35 percent of their time charting in the EHR[4] and physicians devoting sixteen minutes per patient visit to EHR interactions.[5]

Another pressing concern for healthcare professionals is the prospect of job displacement. The integration of automation and AI into healthcare raises concerns that certain tasks currently performed by healthcare workers may become automated, leading to a reduced demand for specific roles. For example, Ohio Health in Central Ohio eliminated 637 information technology and revenue cycle jobs in July of 2022 due to automation.[6]

As AI becomes more pervasive, it may result in an overwhelming abundance of information, creating tension between the healthcare workforce and the public. Clinicians often express frustration with patients' self-diagnosing through internet searches, colloquially referred to as "Dr. Google." Recent data shows a shift from Google to consulting AI, like ChatGPT, for diagnoses when feeling unwell.[7] Differences in opinion arising from this trend can lead to tension between patients and clinicians.

The speed of innovation necessitates recognition of the challenges posed by the rapid pace of technological change in healthcare. Coupled with an aging workforce, individuals may find it challenging to keep up with these changes, or they may simply resist doing so. This could result in potential skills gaps or an exodus of professionals from the workforce.

What Can I Do to Prepare for the Future of Healthcare?

To navigate the future of healthcare effectively, healthcare professionals can adopt the following strategies to maximize their impact:

1. Get Comfortable Being Uncomfortable: Embrace change and adapt to new workflows and technologies, fostering personal and professional growth, as emphasized by Ginni Rometty's quote, "Growth and comfort do not coexist."[8]

2. Stay Informed: Continuously educate yourself about emerging healthcare technologies, trends, and industry developments. Engage with resources such as TED talks, online videos, reputable healthcare journals, conferences, and online courses.

3. Learn New Skills: Pursue opportunities for professional development, certifications, and training to remain current in your field. Consider courses like "Design Thinking for Nurses" by Dr. Marion Leary.[9] The primary authors of this volume, Readinger and Weinstein, are the masters of Diagnostic Design Thinking Groups and offer a wealth of information.[10]

4. Improve Your Digital Literacy: Familiarity with technology is crucial in modern healthcare. Leverage professional development opportunities to fulfill your annual continuing education requirements.

5. Develop a Strong EQ: Enhance empathy and cultivate your emotional quotient (EQ), a vital attribute in healthcare.

6. Network: Recognize the significance of networking as a valuable, yet often overlooked, skill within the healthcare workforce.

What Can I Do to Influence the Future of Healthcare?

To exert a positive influence on the future of healthcare, individuals can take proactive steps to drive change:

1. Speak Up: Use your voice to transform ideas into actions.
2. Practice Collective Ambition: Identify problems and actively work toward solutions.
3. Advocate for Policy Change: Share your expertise to effect change.
4. Mentor the Next Generation: Contribute to the development of future healthcare professionals.
5. Promote Health Equity: Be a voice for marginalized populations and advocate for equitable healthcare access.
6. Engage in Healthcare Technology: Take part in shaping the technological landscape rather than allowing others to dictate it.

The future of healthcare results from innovation and the actions of individuals within the healthcare workforce. Embracing discomfort and practicing collective ambition enables healthcare professionals to positively shape healthcare's evolution for the benefit of patients and communities alike.

Chapter 9

Inspiring Gen Z to Stay

Nicole George

As a profession, we must fully reflect on the tumultuous, unprecedented times that were the COVID-19 pandemic. We endured the initial days of uncertainty, unsure of the sources for personal protective equipment (PPE), ventilators, or even the availability of nurses themselves. We were challenged daily—mentally, physically, and emotionally. We also witnessed our profession undergo a rapid transformation in how our workforce was staffed, trained, recruited, and retained. Never in our lifetime have we seen such systemic, rapid change in our profession.

Data from the National Database for Nursing Quality Indicators® (NDNQI)[1] shows a steady year-over-year decline in nursing engagement in most hospitals within the United States. The Advisory Board reports the national turnover rate for clinical nurses reached 27.1 percent during 2021 and only slightly decreased to 22.5 percent in 2022.[2] These tremendously high turnover rates dealt blows to hospital budgets, quality of care, and registered nurse (RN) engagement.

So, how do we inspire nurses to stay?

We inspire nurses to stay by ensuring that their fundamental needs are *consistently* met. Nurses and organizational leaders must recognize that needs vary from generation to generation. Leaders must know that the newest generation of nurses (Generation Z , or "Gen Z") have and will continue to enter the workforce over the decade and beyond.

What We Know about Gen Z

Gen Z was born between the years 1995 and 2012. The oldest of this generation has been part of the nursing workforce since about 2015. Gen Z has grown up in uncertain times as relates to economics, culture, and public violence, leading to concerns about their financial, social, and physical security. Gen Z also values when individuals in their circles are available, transparent, promote instant gratification, and give meaningful recognition.[3] Lastly, and likely most notable, Gen Z is very tech savvy—the first generation to grow up as "digital natives." This generation is also more likely to advocate for and support issues they feel are important (or to simply voice their opinions) via social media. Being a digital native aligns with the expectation of instant gratification.[4]

The COVID-19 Pandemic's Effect on the Newest Generation of Nurses

The COVID-19 pandemic overwhelmed many healthcare organizations as several Gen Z cohorts entered the workforce. Those Gen Z nurses did not have the crucial opportunity to attend clinicals and harness their skills. During the COVID-19 pandemic, Gen Z nurses faced unprecedented, unchartered, and uncertain times. With limited resources, this generation was heavily influenced by the cultural and social factors that upended healthcare during the pandemic.

Data show Gen Z had increased levels of anxiety, depression, and suicidal ideation.[5]

Meeting the Needs of Gen Z Nurses

To ensure that the needs of the newest generation of nurses are met, nurse leaders must consider Maslow's Hierarchy of Needs while developing initiatives and action plans. Tailoring Maslow's theory to each generation is important but will be particularly key to ensure that the needs of Gen Z are met. Physiological needs are what Maslow theorized to be the most foundational—if these needs are not met, an individual will not be able to tend to needs noted higher in the hierarchy.

Nurse leaders are charged with ensuring that the *psychological* needs of Gen Z nurses are met consistently. How then do we inspire them to stay? Nurse leaders must ensure that the nurse practice environment is conducive to high engagement and psychological safety.

Nurse Leader Support

One of the most effective practices a nurse leader can implement to promote high engagement is active and continuous listening. This can be done both formally and informally. Nurse leaders formally listen through nurse engagement surveys, both full and pulse surveys. Organizations must have a standardized approach as to how nurse leaders analyze and act on the data. The nurse leader must follow through on the expectations set by the organization and be held accountable for subsequent action plans. Informally, nurse leaders must listen when spending time with their teams; it is important that all nurses feel they have access to their nurse leaders and that the nurse leader is responsive. However, for Gen Z nurses, access to and responsiveness from their nurse leaders are of the utmost importance. During nurse leader rounding, nurse leaders can address questions or concerns while being transparent, providing instant feedback, and meaningful recognition where appropriate.

Addressing the Mental Health of Gen Z Nurses

Mental health issues have affected all generations since the COVID-19 pandemic; nevertheless, it's worth noting that Gen Z in particular has experienced heightened levels of anxiety, depression, and suicidal ideation.[6] Organizations must first make certain that they cultivate a culture of psychological safety and address any stigmas that may exist related to the mental health of all employees. Specific to Gen Z nurses, nurse leaders must foster a sense of psychological safety. Employee assistance programs (EAPs) must be discussed in an open, non-stigmatized manner. Nurse leaders must also speak about access- ing available mental health resources openly during huddles, staff meetings, and rounding. When organization-wide mental health initia- tives are rolled out, nurse leaders must work diligently to dismantle stigma associated with taking part in such programs. Such stigma may prevent a Gen Z nurse from speaking up about their own mental health and accessing available resources. If your organization does not have mental health resources available for employees, advocate for these! The mental health of all our nurses is vital to ensuring a healthy workforce for our collective future.

Looking Forward and Doubling Down on Inspiration

As of this writing, the future nurses of Gen Z are still in elementary school! They are likely to exhibit different attributes from their older generational counterparts. The looming question is, "How will the future workforce look?" The COVID-19 pandemic has exacerbated the shortage and projections show that we may lose nearly half a million nurses in the next two years. Inspiring all nurses to stay is particularly important, but we must also ensure our profession remains attractive to those who have yet to graduate high school. Hospitals are competing with industries that provide competitive salaries, benefits, and remote work—this would be ideal for any generation! However, in addition to keeping our finger on the pulse of today (and working to tackle today's challenges), we must also keep the future in mind. Partner with your local schools and speak about our profession at career days. Work diligently as a nurse leader to advocate for similar benefits that exist elsewhere in the healthcare industry. Lastly, remember why *you* became a nurse and reconnect with your "why" regularly. Encourage this practice with your nursing teams. We will continue to move forward as a profession one day at a time, but keeping our own why at the center will keep us connected to our mission as nurses.

Part Two

Well-Being

The metaphor of securing our own oxygen masks before assisting others resonates not just in the friendly skies, but also in the journey of work and life. Today's leaders realize that younger generations of workers, including Millennials and Gen Z, prioritize health and seek more fulfillment from work. These generations expect support in coping with the diverse stressors they encounter at home and in the workplace. Frontline workers, particularly in healthcare, lack the flexibility enjoyed by their counterparts in other industries, leading to burnout, staffing challenges, emotional stress, and so much more.

While the term "work-life balance" is often mentioned, what nurses really want are work-life boundaries! Many of our nurse colleagues silently endure pain, struggles, and feelings of despair.

Stress takes a toll on both our minds and our bodies. Clearly, we can reap significant benefits from reducing the stress in our lives at work and at home. Life gets in the way, and boundaries seem impossible.

Work-life balance is a barometer for well-being—and for becoming the best version of you. Supporting nurses' well-being is now more crucial than ever, as it enables them to fulfill their duties and enhances their connections with patients. Join us as we embark on the well-being express—one replete with success stories, tips, and techniques that demonstrate how and why staff well-being is essential in the realm of healthcare. Life is a balancing act, and the pursuit of balance begins here and now!

Chapter 10

Workforce Challenges . . . Old News or New?

Vicki Good

Is the depleted nursing workforce something new? Absolutely not—this is old news. We have all experienced fluctuations in staffing, which can compromise patients and caregivers alike. What makes today's workforce situation different? While history repeats itself, research reveals this shortage to be more than cyclical. Both the Advisory Board[1] and McKinsey & Company[2] surveyed frontline nurses and found that the reasons nurses leave the profession relate to a compromised work environment, burnout, and overall dissatisfaction. Nursing vacancy rates are prolific and may be attributed to declining workforce numbers, increasing retirements, psychologically unsafe work environments, and the demands of the profession.

Burnout, likewise, is not new. From an individual standpoint, pandemic-related burnout is "to blame," but the concern is ongoing.[3] According to Maslach,[4] burnout syndrome develops in the face of exhaustion (emotional and physical), depersonalization, and lack of the feeling of making a difference. Post-pandemic, burnout rates have escalated to as high as 60 percent.[5,6] In completed research involving multidisciplinary professionals, the findings confirm that burnout continues to challenge us. For nurses, burnout is a driver of quiet quitting. The United States continues to see critical nursing vacancies, with rates exceeding 15 percent nationally and exceeding 25 percent in some areas.[7] While we cannot eliminate burnout, leaders can play an incremental role in generating improvement that has lasting impacts.

A Healthy Work Environment

The health of the work environment directly affects the health of the workforce. Burnout syndrome includes internal/individual and external/environmental factors. External factors affect stress levels. Internal factors include the ability to practice resilience, a much-needed response to that stress. *The Lancet* published a meta-analysis on which interventions—those that target the individual or those that target the environment—are best to prevent burnout syndrome.[8] They found that both types of interventions must be pursued to effectively combat burnout. A similar meta-analysis proved that the strongest evidence for preventing burnout syndrome is implementing organizational-directed interventions.[9] An unhealthy work environment can negatively impact all clinicians, including those with strong resiliency skills. Post-pandemic nursing studies show similar findings.

In response to workforce concerns, surveys have been conducted post-pandemic to detail the needs of frontline nurses. The key marker is the workplace itself. Needs identified by nurses include support to ensure that all clinicians can take breaks without interruption,[10] a safe environment, and the ability for nurses to do doing meaningful work, including mechanisms for nurses to be listened to and supported. A survey of over nine thousand critical care nurses reported that the health of the work environment has declined over the last three years; less than 70 percent of the surveyed nurses reported that their organization addressed the health of the work environment.[11] The numbers are telling, and today's leaders feel overwhelmed with the task at hand; they lack a starting point.

The obvious first step is facilitating a healthy work environment. As Martin Luther King Jr. said, "Take the first step, you don't have to see the whole staircase, just take the first step." Nurses are committed partners, and they need leaders that are equally committed to setting up a work environment in which a nurse thrives. The survey discussed above[12] reveals that when leaders address the work environment, the nurse has a positive perception of that environment and a lower desire to leave the unit.

In 2005, the American Association of Critical Care Nurses (AACN)[13] defined six standards for setting up and supporting a healthy work environment. Supported by evidence, these hallmark standards have remained consistent over time and have been adopted by many organizations. The standards include skilled communication, true collaboration, effective decision-making, proper staffing, meaningful recognition, and authentic leadership. Each of the standards is important; they are essential and work synergistically to contribute to a healthy work environment.

Addressing all six standards at one time can be a daunting task; begin with the one that is most challenging for your team. Dialogue with the team to access what is important to them. Reestablishing trust between leaders and frontline nurses, which has declined in recent times, is critical to addressing work environment concerns.[14] Knowing the needs of the workforce, what is one step that can result in positive outcomes? One common desire of nurses is flexibility. Flexibility presents itself in many ways. Variations in scheduling (full-time versus gig), employment status, benefit packages, and innovative care delivery models are just a few examples.[15]

Redesign

We now have a greater demand for care and fewer human resources to deliver it.[16] An innovative redesign of the care delivery model is needed more than ever. The solutions must involve the input of front-line nurses. Through the years, nurses have taken on many non-nursing functions, but nurses have a fervent desire to return to the fundamental calling of nursing: caring for patients. Care model redesign must focus the nurse's time on the patient and their professional growth.[17,18]

Nursing's future is dependent on addressing the work environment and improving the care delivery model. The nursing profession has had cyclical challenges through the years; each time the profession has survived and thrived.

Looking back, what would I tell a younger version of me? Keep laser focused on the work environment. As a leader, sustaining a healthy work environment is imperative for our current and future workforce. Working in a healthy work environment is fundamental in keeping a thriving nursing workforce.

Chapter 11

Wellness Cultures to Improve Population Health and Well-Being in Institutions of Higher Learning and Academic Medical Centers, The Ohio State Solution

Bernadette Mazurek Melnyk and Megan Amaya

There is currently a mental health pandemic blooming out of the COVID-19 pandemic. Rates of depression and anxiety have skyrocketed. Many people attempted to cope with COVID-19 by engaging in unhealthy behaviors, such as emotional eating and increases in alcohol and drug use.[1,2] Further, 60 percent of Americans have a chronic condition, yet 80 percent of chronic disease is totally preventable with a few healthy lifestyle behaviors, such as thirty minutes of physical activity, five fruits and vegetables per day, not smoking, limiting alcohol intake to one standard drink a day if alcohol is consumed, sleeping at least seven hours a night, and practicing stress reduction.[3]

A National Plan

More universities and academic medical centers are hiring chief wellness officers to spearhead improvements in population health and well-being so that their faculty, clinicians, staff, and students are healthy, happy, engaged, and productive. This is especially important given that approximately 35 to 60 percent of the workforce is currently experiencing burnout, which is strongly associated with depression and anxiety.[4] Burnout in clinicians costs the United States healthcare system $4.6 billion annually and adversely impacts the quality and safety of care, which compromises patient outcomes.[5] The National Academy of Medicine (NAM) launched its action collaborative on clinician well-being and resilience in 2017.[6] In October 2022, NAM released its *National Plan for Health Workforce Well-Being* with the following recommendations:

- Create and sustain positive work and learning environments and culture.
- Invest in measurement and assessment strategies and research.
- Support mental health and decrease stigma.
- Address compliance, regulatory, and policy barriers for daily work.
- Engage effective technology tools.
- Institutionalize well-being as a long-term value.
- Recruit and retain a diverse and inclusive workforce.

The Ohio State University Solution

The Ohio State University was the first institution of higher learning to appoint a chief wellness officer, Dr. Bernadette Melnyk, in 2012.[7] Since then, this large Midwestern public land grant university, which houses an academic health center with seven hospitals, has established an ambitious wellness strategic plan with a vision to become the healthiest university and community on the globe.[8] The strategic plan instituted efforts to build and sustain a robust wellness structure and comprehensive multi-component strategy that targets evidence-based interventions from top leaders to middle managers and supervisors to the grassroots people in the organization, all while focusing on building and sustaining a wellness culture and environment that makes healthy behaviors the default in the organization.[9]

Culture eats strategy for breakfast, lunch, and dinner; it affects how people feel and how they behave. Perceived wellness culture and environment is strongly associated with both mental health outcomes and healthy lifestyle behaviors.[10,11] Therefore, at Ohio State, as part of its evidence-based quality improvement approach to improving population health and well-being, wellness culture is measured annually along with ten leading modifiable health indicators that account for 25 percent of healthcare spending (e.g., blood pressure, body mass index, physical activity, depression, anxiety). Deidentified anonymous data from annual faculty and staff personal health assessments and biometric screenings are then shared with college and unit vice presidents and their executive teams so that strategies can be implemented to improve where needed.

At Ohio State, there are hundreds of units and departments that exist on the academic and medical center sides of the university, as well as in regional, satellite, and county extension settings. It is important for the wellness team to collaborate with employees in these subcultures to meet their wellness needs and create a sustainable overall culture of wellness. Grassroots efforts, such as wellness champions, are a low-cost but extremely effective strategy in helping to create a culture of well-being throughout an organization.[12] The wellness champion initiative at Ohio State is called the Buckeye Wellness Innovator (BWI) program. The Ohio State University has seven hundred faculty and staff BWIs who work with the chief wellness officer's Buckeye Wellness team to help build a culture of wellness at the department/unit level. The BWI program provides opportunities for intrinsically motivated faculty and staff to share their passion for wellness and inspire their colleagues to live healthier lives through supporting peer adoption and maintenance of health-promoting behaviors.[13]

BWIs handle communicating health and wellness information and activities to their colleagues, motivating and encouraging colleagues to participate in wellness initiatives, and planning and implementing targeted wellness activities and programs in their respective departments. Serving as a visible, approachable, and enthusiastic leader of wellness initiatives in their department, a BWI devotes a minimum of two to three hours per month to fulfilling their role and responsibilities. The fulfillment of these requirements during paid work hours is at the discretion of their direct manager or supervisor. More information about the BWI program can be found in previously published articles.[14,15]

BWIs consistently serve as inspirational role models of health and wellness practices, both personally and professionally. The Buckeye Wellness program facilitators provide BWIs with the training, materials, resources, examples, funding opportunities, and ongoing support that enable them to organize meaningful wellness programs that resonate with and meet the needs of their colleagues. Small grants are competitively funded that enable the BWIs to offer programming and build other resources to improve health and well-being in their units. BWIs provide cues and reminders for engaging in healthy habits throughout the workday, and they build a resolute team that supports their colleagues' engagement in health-promoting habits.[16,17]

Each year, a quality improvement survey is administered to all BWIs to collect information on what types of activities the BWIs are planning and implementing, which dimensions of wellness they promote the most, and the various successful efforts, needs, and barriers to implementation that may have come up. From there, data is shared with wellness program stakeholders. Participation in the program is tracked annually, as well as fiscal resources needed to administer the program. There is a BWI advisory committee, composed of existing BWIs, that provides feedback and information to better help program facilitators meet the needs of BWIs across the university. BWIs also have access to a resource-rich "champion corner," an online portal where they can locate materials and items (e.g., fliers, points of contact) they may need to fulfill their role. BWIs are a low-cost yet high-impact strategy that enhances wellness cultures in the grassroots of the organization.

The Evidence Base

In addition to the strategies mentioned above, it is critical to have a menu of evidence-based wellness programs available for faculty, clinicians, staff, and students. At Ohio State, programming is offered to target the ten dimensions of wellness: career, creative, digital, emotional, environmental, financial, intellectual, physical, social, and spiritual wellness. Decreasing stigma about seeking mental health services if needed is critical, along with evidence-based prevention programs to build mental resiliency, such as mindfulness and cognitive behavioral skills building, which are supported by a strong body of research that demonstrates they reduce anxiety and depression.

Finally, system issues that are at the root cause of burnout must be fixed, such as work overload, understaffing, too many unnecessary bureaucratic tasks, and problems with the electronic medical record. Only when a comprehensive multi-component strategy is implemented that includes an evidence-based quality improvement approach that builds and sustains a culture of wellness will population health and well-being outcomes improve.

Reflection

Although there will always be a tremendous need for high-quality sick and crisis care, a paradigm shift to wellness and prevention is needed for a healthier America. We at The Ohio State University are leading the way.

Chapter 12

Making Well-Being a Reality . . . at the Intersection of Well-Being and Equity

Sue Johnson

The pandemic taught us some painful lessons. Nurses were on the frontlines of the battle against the virus, initially with inadequate personal protective equipment (PPE), on unfamiliar units with different team members, and dealing with life-threatening crises and multiple patient deaths. At the onset, nurses and healthcare personnel were heroes to the public, but as time wore on, that changed. Misinformation transformed nurses into opponents for promoting vaccinations and masking. As the third year of the pandemic ends, nurses are still considered the most trusted profession (for the twenty-second year), but the 79 percent exceedingly high or high rating for nurses in 2023 is the lowest percentage since 2014.[1] Gallup interviewed 1,020 US adults from all fifty states and the District of Columbia between November 9 and December 2, 2022. Nursing's trust score dropped 10 percent after the pandemic, reflecting negativity and partisan differences in the country. The next closest professions are physicians at 62 percent and pharmacists at 58 percent.[2]

Three years of constant stress has changed nursing practice and nurses themselves. Burnout, secondary traumatic stress, and moral injury have contributed to nurses leaving their positions and even the profession itself. The risk of nurse suicide has also been exacerbated by the pandemic. Much of the focus has been on reducing stress and burnout while fostering resilience. Well-being has lacked clear definition, and organizations and nurses themselves have struggled to find successful approaches to achieve it.[3]

Well-being goes beyond simply avoiding burnout and is not solely the responsibility of individual nurses. Organizations are accountable for, and should actively contribute to the well-being of nurses, playing a crucial role in fostering a healthy work environment.

Let's start by defining well-being: "Nurse well-being at work is a nurse's positive evaluation of oneself and one's contributions to the work of nursing. It allows the individual nurse to be the best whole person mentally, physically, emotionally, and spiritually they can be at any given point in time and the ability to adapt and overcome adversity to the extent possible."[4]

For nurses to achieve well-being at work, organizations must:

- Establish and maintain programs and processes for well-being that are readily accessible to nurses and other health team members.
- Supply adequate resources to carry out the work.
- Provide a supportive, positive culture.
- Empower nurse leaders to support frontline staff members in crisis situations.
- Ensure high-quality communication, transparency, and psychological safety.
- Supply education and training opportunities.
- Include nurses in decisions about their work.

- Support the physical needs of the nursing staff—nutrition, hydration, meal breaks, adequate rest periods, and safety (physical, psychological, and mental).
- Restore joy in the workplace.[5]

The effect of equity on well-being—positive or negative—must also be addressed by healthcare organizations and nurses themselves. Lack of equity adversely impacts well-being for everyone, regardless of their racial, gender, and ethnic backgrounds. Prejudice and discrimination continue to exist although many healthcare facilities have established DEI (diversity, equity, and inclusivity) programs. We all have biases, and implicit bias is a result of our upbringing. These biases must be addressed to truly achieve equity and well-being for all nurses and other healthcare team members.[6]

Organizations can address equity for well-being by:

- role modeling diversity, equity, and inclusivity as a daily expectation;
- demonstrating zero tolerance for prejudice and discrimination;
- supplying ongoing education about confronting biases; and
- welcoming nurses representing the communities they serve at decision-making tables.[7]

Nurses themselves also have a role to play in their own well-being. We must explore our own implicit bias and grow in allyship of individuals unlike ourselves. We must transform relationships with our colleagues from all demographics—women and men, Black, Hispanic, Asian, Native American, LGBTQIA+—to learn from them and support everyone's growth as a team. Equity and well-being should go hand in hand as we serve as role models for change.

The American Nurses Association (ANA) created the Healthy Nurse, Healthy Nation program prior to the pandemic to improve the health of US nurses—one nurse at a time. The program uses a web platform to supply resources and content for nurses designed to inspire action in six domains: physical activity, rest, safety, nutrition, mental health, and quality of life. Nurses are engaged with the goal of creating a healthy nurse population that will translate into a healthier workforce that will sustain safe, effective healthcare. This free service is available to all nurses.[8]

Another approach nurses can use to enhance their well-being is a tool called Three Good Things. Each nurse should write down three good things at the end of each day. This simple act can improve happiness and well-being that can be sustained for six months, according to one study.[9]

It's important to remember that well-being is different for each of us. For some, it's practicing mindfulness and coping strategies. For others, it's writing and journaling. Still others need peer support, collegial relationships, education and growth opportunities, and purposeful work where they can accomplish their goals. Each of us should self-reflect and engage in activities that enable us "to be the best whole person mentally, physically, emotionally, and spiritually" for our own well-being.[10]

Stress and trauma will continue to exist in the future, but you have an opportunity to engage in post-traumatic growth rather than post-traumatic stress. Nursing faces many challenges, and we must care for ourselves and our colleagues to meet these challenges. Well-being is essential to professional success. With the support of our organizations, our colleagues, and ourselves we can truly be the best we can be in our professional and personal lives. You deserve no less!

Chapter 13

Positivity and Purpose . . . the Path to Well-Being

Sheila Anne Burke*

Can positivity and purpose ensure a healthy workforce? Today's nursing profession is in a crisis state. Record numbers of nurses are leaving the profession, and they do not intend to return. Fewer students are entering nursing education programs, and those programs are more intense as students have so much more to learn. Students struggle to meet the requirements for entry, and once admitted, the rigors of the curriculum, the clinical requirements, and the demands of the profession itself lead to attrition.

From unstable and complex work environments to incivility, nurses and other healthcare professionals are at a higher risk each day for losing their sense of overall well-being. Tensions are high. The new graduate may lack confidence in their ability and worry about performance and productivity. Inadequate staffing may result in poor outcomes, low satisfaction scores, and burnout.

---

* Sheila Anne Burke sadly passed away on March 30, 2024.

When nurses question their positivity and purpose, we all lose. The health system loses due to recruitment and retention issues. The patient loses due to the potential risk of errors from stressed caregivers who may lack focus during an acute clinical situation. Team members lose due to lack of collaboration and accountability. Present-day nurses contend with demanding workloads, insufficient support, moral distress, and mental health challenges. Healthcare systems across the US are challenged by the complex circumstances and the risks we face each day.

Impact of the Pandemic

Less than two years after the onset, the COVID-19 pandemic had dramatically and permanently affected the entire world. We realized that life as it existed before the pandemic had to change. Unable to respond adequately to the dramatic need for increased science, training, and resources that developed as COVID-19 traumatized society and healthcare specifically, our resources were taxed, and our systems suffered.

The Role of Well-Being

Pre-pandemic, there was growth in the use of wellness programs, but the severity and extended disruption of what had been life "pre-COVID-19" revealed the need for increased deliberate development of wellness and health promotion initiatives that would create positive change. While the healthcare community had been aware of the social determinants of health prior to COVID-19, the pandemic highlighted tremendous disparities and access issues. Since the pandemic, there is new awareness of the effects of isolation and gaps in access. One of the most alarming developments has been the unparalleled increase in violence and the escalation of senseless murders. This has created a sense of pervasive and exhausting anxiety. In the US, gun violence rose at an incredible rate and continues to be a threat to well-being in a way that damages entire communities.

A major step that would revolutionize the healthcare system and affect our recruitment and retention efforts would be the inclusion of proven wellness strategies within our clinical and academic settings. This might include integrating a selection of evidence-based modalities and organizational systems that promote well-being through mindfulness training, health behavior support, and work environments that would honor well-being. We have long been aware of the positive outcomes this approach can bring.

The mental health issues that have become a national concern can be addressed. By incorporating (hard wiring) well-being support strategies into work environments, it is possible to shape improved outcomes for the nurses who face the tremendous stress of caregiving in their current practice settings. One resource that has a wealth of material is the National Institute of Mental Health (NIMH),[1] whose mission is to transform the understanding and treatment of mental illness through research, paving the way for prevention, recovery, and cure.

Self-Care

Self-care is a key factor in well-being. Nurses must individually and collectively own the responsibility for self-care! Nurses can lead the way, and benefit from, a focus on making well-being a priority within our hospitals and health systems. Awareness of one's stress triggers is a good starting point; recognizing the need for help and knowing where and how to seek it are critical next steps. Components of a healthy work environment include an infrastructure that fosters healing intention, personal wholeness, healthy relationships and lifestyles, and sustainability. Healthcare systems need to support these elements within their organizations.

The Future

The future is shaped by our beliefs and the actions we manifest. In all its history, nursing has at times shown creativity, courage, and initiative. The path to well-being is to honor the nursing values of holistic healthcare and the importance of prevention and health promotion instead of a disease-management model. Well-being in the future will require nurses who are prepared to use the science of well-being, available and emerging technologies, and the awareness that as a profession, nursing needs to nurture its own well-being.

As a profession, nurses can be better advocates for themselves and push for healthy and health-promoting work environments.[2] Nursing can use the resources that exist to set up a national well-being agenda. Leaders in national and international healthcare organizations will pay attention if evidence proves the benefits. Nurse leaders, nurse researchers, nurse educators, and those who work in holistic nursing are all potential collaborators in advancing the concepts of positivity and purpose—potentially changing and enriching our chosen profession.

Reflection

When I entered the nursing profession, the idea of wellness was transformed as innovative approaches attracted US consciousness. At the time, there was considerable resistance in many areas of Western medicine to what were considered radical initiatives, which included yoga, acupuncture, massage therapy, aromatherapy, and meditation. Today, these and many other approaches are recognized as having value and evidence-based support. If I was beginning my career today, there are three things I would do related to well-being: 1) I would focus on familiarizing myself with the research. 2) I would pursue information about well-being that is grounded in science and avoid being influenced by marketing or social media trends. 3) I would accept responsibility for my own well-being.

In the early years of my career, it was common to earn recognition by working extreme hours and being "self-sacrificing"—going for extended periods without sleep, food, or exercise. In recent years this is changing, and more organizations are realizing the importance of healthy lifestyles. I would be mindful of making my wellness a priority and supporting health-promoting behaviors in my practice area. I would align with other members of the healthcare workforce to promote wellness through initiatives that increase well-being in populations at risk.

Today, I work as a volunteer with the Alzheimer's Association to educate communities about the resources and support that can improve the well-being of those living with Alzheimer's and related dementias. This activity allows me to empower people by supplying strategies for creating well-being in their lives, even in the face of this challenging situation. This work reinforces my positivity and restores my purpose; it allows me to be of service along the path to well-being.

Chapter 14

Broken Promises vs. Broken Systems

Katie Boston-Leary

Healthy Nurse, Healthy Nation

The actors on the main stage—nurses, physicians, and other health-care professionals—display a spectrum of emotions, ranging from profound hurt and pain to fleeting moments of joy, providing audiences with a poignant and compelling experience. But the emotions being shared are not merely for entertainment; they serve as a catalyst to inspire action and urgent change toward sustained improvement.

The motto for Healthy Nurse, Healthy Nation is "improving the nation's health, one nurse at a time." This was based on the starfish method. We strive to remain undaunted by the enormous task at hand, but we continue to take our small wins and celebrate milestones on the way to meeting our big hairy audacious goal (BHAG) to improve nurses' health. Focusing on improving the health of the nation's 5.3 million nurses should in turn have a positive impact on population health.

Are we having any impact or making any inroads? It is hard to tell when we have a constantly moving target. We are dealing with a growing aging population, increasing acuity, a nurse staffing crisis, widening health disparities, and ballooning healthcare spending with marginal outcomes. Despite all these challenges, we are still encouraged by the stories from nurses in the Healthy Nurse, Healthy Nation program about how they have not only improved their own health but also pay it forward within their communities at work, at home, and on social media.

Invariably, the system will remain broken until we focus on improving nurses' health and well-being. Addressing nurses' well-being requires unrelenting focus on the unhealthy environments where nurses practice and function. The physical, cognitive, and emotional workload and burdens that nurses must carry require herculean effort, will, grit, and grace. Grace entails the emotional will and fortitude for nurses to forgive and temporarily forget; they must if they are going to do it all again day after day, hoping that someone is listening who will help make it better.

Albert Einstein said that you cannot use an old map to explore a new world. The new maps that are needed to navigate a new world of care delivery are still in development. Until we implement and invest in this space, nurses' well-being will continue to be compromised. The Pulse of the Nation's 2022 nurses survey[1] showed that there was a strong link between staffing and nurses' well-being. The issue at hand is not only about having experienced nurses but also about patient acuity, intensity, expertise, relevant competency, and models to reduce workload.

Our care delivery models are dated and under-researched. The delayed response to evolving these models has now resulted in nurses becoming the organizational sponge for responsibilities that were previously and should still be managed elsewhere. A newly graduated nurse who had enjoyed careers in several other industries told me recently that she had never had a role where so much was constantly needed and expected from a single human being within a ten-to-twelve-hour shift.

Think-Tank Approach

The Partners for Nurse Staffing Think Tank[2] members defined innovative care delivery as establishing models that combine high tech and high touch for high-quality care with an inclusive and integrated approach for patient and nurse satisfaction, reduction of practice pain points, and improved outcomes. A tribrid approach to care requires boots on the ground, virtual nursing, and tech-enabled care to reduce workload. It is time to implement technology that works for nurses and not the other way around. The tail should not wag the dog.

Humility and Wisdom . . . a Winning Combination

Humility is needed for proper action to lead to healing. That means humility for us as leaders to accept our missteps, miscalculations, and misappropriations; and it means humility to accept that we may need to look for new answers to old, perennial, and wicked problems.

After humility comes the wisdom to apply lessons learned, wisdom that obeys the signal for a renewed way of caring for patients and the teams we lead. We must be relentless in our efforts to prioritize and allocate resources to test new models of care and to stay the course to build a positive future for nursing. Leaders must also realize that their teams want to be led and supported differently. Wisdom opens the door to new opportunities to process things differently with innovative ideas and insights that align with the needs of today's worker. Traditionalists tend to play it safe, to hold on to old ideas and ways of leading, and to ignore the new and emerging reality. Wisdom will forge novel approaches to leading if it results from continuous engagement with internal and external stakeholders and staying evidence informed.

Reflection

We must recognize that the system we operate within is shaped by the condition of the people within it, and conversely, the state of the system influences the individuals within it. Is the system broken because the people that operate within it are broken? Or are people breaking due to the broken system? Nurses will tell you that they are not breaking but they are broken, and this is in part due to broken promises from leaders. A healthy work environment is fertile ground to attract and maintain healthy nurses and healthcare professionals.

A wise person told me that leadership is about managing the present, selectively forgetting the past, and most importantly, creating a new future. Our growth comes with being open to learn and listen while crafting a shared vision for teams to want to be a part of. This is the "new possible" that we should eagerly and urgently create for nursing. This approach replaces the traditional workplace hierarchy with models that are more flexible and responsive, built on higher levels of connection. In this approach, organizations work together with their people to create personalized, authentic, and motivating experiences that strengthen individual, team, and organizational performance. We must evolve ourselves from being managers to becoming neuro-leaders who are idea seekers, future creators, upper-brain focused, vulnerable, and taking direction from several sources. It is time to activate tomorrow's leaders today!

Chapter 15

Frontline Nurses . . . Experiencing Well-Being

Anna Dermenchyan

Challenges Facing our Profession Today

> *"Healthcare is rapidly changing, and this constant change*
> *offers us opportunities to step up, lean in, and showcase*
> *our problem-solving skills and leadership abilities."*
> –A. Dermenchyan

We face many challenges in healthcare today, including burnout and low levels of staffing. We have seen how the pandemic significantly increased fatigue, stress, anxiety, depression, post-traumatic stress disorder (PTSD), moral distress, compassion fatigue, and suicide.[1] Already overworked and underappreciated prior to the pandemic, increased workloads and a lack of predictability overwhelmed and exhausted frontline nurses. Nurse well-being fell to the back burner!

The height of the pandemic brought a mass exodus of nurses from units caring for COVID-19 patients; many nurses transferred to less acute clinical practices. Those who practiced in unhealthy work environments, where they lacked support from colleagues and leadership, experienced burnout and wanted to leave the profession altogether.[2] Pre-pandemic, there was some semblance of balance between work and personal life, but the pandemic introduced added stressors for our colleagues with children and elderly parents. Many nurses were stretched thin in their roles as caregivers. Overwhelm and exhaustion led to burnout. Demands for nurses' time reached impossible levels due to increased acuity, a high census, and limited staffing. The work was never done.

Around one hundred thousand nurses left the workforce during the pandemic, and studies reveal that eight hundred thousand nurses say they intend to leave the workforce by 2027.[3]

Disruptions to pre-licensure nursing education and comparable declines among nursing support staff resulted in turnover to the point of a major staffing crisis. Insufficient nurse staffing is a pervasive threat to quality, safety, and nurse well-being.

Trends That Have Changed Healthcare

"Let's support and value frontline nurses. We will all need care one day."

–A. Dermenchyan

Nurses were celebrated as heroes during a crisis, yet were not given the necessary support and resources to thrive as a profession. Prior to the pandemic, there was a lack of understanding about the multifaceted role of nurses. Media coverage showed the public that nursing care is indispensable in hospitals and ambulatory care centers. Nurses were sometimes the only ones at the patient's bedside during their hospital stay.

As the first line of defense for responding to public health crises, nurses have valuable expertise and perspectives to offer from the frontlines. Yet, we are often missing from important decision-making tables that affect our lives and work. We need a voice in government, health-related commissions, panels, and task forces to help improve healthcare.[4] Nurses' foundational commitment is to patient health—not cost, politics, shareholders, profits, appearances, or other competing incentives in healthcare. The unique perspective of nurses is needed to improve health and ensure an efficient and effective healthcare system at all levels of care.

Leaders Building a Healthy Workforce for Our Collective Future

"I believe in the power of nurses and using our bold voices to make a difference in the lives of patients and their families, as well as our communities, countries, and the world."

–A. Dermenchyan

Healthcare leaders must prioritize providing a work environment that upholds Maslow's Hierarchy of Needs to create wellness and a culture of safety. Nurses must believe that their physiological and safety needs are met. Leaders must offer their staff a zero-tolerance policy toward workplace violence. Nurses in all settings must collaborate to create a culture of respect free of incivility, bullying, and workplace violence.[5] When basic levels of need are met, nurses can have a sense of belonging and feel more ownership in their work. When nurses fully engage in their work and function at their highest level, they give their full attention to their patients and organizations.

Just-in-time leadership support is crucial in a time of crisis. During the pandemic, areas where leadership was present through rounding and daily communication updates provided visibility and support for nurses. An expert hotline that supplied the latest science/evidence on the most up-to-date work guidance, as well as peer support and referrals to mental health resources, was invaluable. For units facing stress, loss, or difficulty, initiatives such as Tea for the Soul from the pastoral care department can offer support and a sense of true teamwork through one-hour sessions to unwind and have tea and cookies.[6] Hosting Schwartz Center Rounds as a structured way to supply a safe forum to discuss the distressing experiences that nurses and other members of the healthcare team are going through helps create a support community.[7] Urban Zen and other wellness programs have the potential to help heal the entire healthcare community through the tools of mindfulness, yoga, Reiki, and essential oils.[8]

Leaders can incorporate practical solutions to reduce medical errors through stress reduction for nurses.[9] Policies limiting the number of overtime shifts and role modeling self-care behaviors and cultures of self-care are beneficial. Added resource staff, such as a full-time resource nurse, can help the unit with clinical duties such as quality checks, giving breaks to other nurses, or admissions. While supplying break relief, the resource nurse can do quality and safety checks to support the primary nurse and supply peer coaching if needed. Finally, leaders can offer meaningful recognition by setting up formal and informal reward and recognition programs that make nurses feel valued. Having systems in place to recognize nurses in an individualized and meaningful way enhances a sense of value, leading to greater nurse engagement.[10]

Ways to Advocate for Nurses and Nursing

*"Healthcare is in a deep state of exhaustion. As a
collective, we need to advocate for our own rights and
stand up for what we believe in."*
                                                    –A. Dermenchyan

Nurses' clinical ability and perspectives offer unique insights into patient care. However, our work is not always visible. The pandemic presented unique opportunities for nurses to showcase our work to the media and public.

We can all support the voice of frontline nurses and advocate for their inclusion. Leaders can mentor nurses by offering opportunities for involvement in various community and leadership activities. For example, working with media teams, a chief nursing officer or dean of a school of nursing can draw attention to the contribution of their nurses and nursing students from the frontlines. Nurses can be celebrated for all the roles they fill.

Reflection

*"Once you find your purpose, you can radically change
your life for the better and impact the lives of your family
and community in the years to come."*
                                                    –A. Dermenchyan

Reflection helps us grow! As a nine-year-old immigrant to the United States, English was not my first language. I struggled in my younger years with confidence and finding my authentic voice. As a new critical care nurse, I often felt stuck in caring for patients with a challenging post-surgical recovery. I was uncomfortable speaking up to the interdisciplinary team about the ethical issues I encountered. When I brought it up with other nurses, I assumed they were hesitant and could not voice their concerns. These experiences propelled me to attend the local ethics conferences to learn about the broader issues that face nursing.

Similar bedside experiences drove me to find opportunities that would help me speak up, build confidence, and make me a stronger advocate for my patients and myself. I attended communication courses to master the delivery of effective messages and build consensus around my goals. As I transitioned from novice to advanced beginner and then competency, I was empowered to champion skilled communication and true collaboration in my unit. Since then, I have taken multiple opportunities to showcase my voice on issues important to healthcare.

I entered nursing with all the idealism for the profession, unprepared for the challenges I met with complex patient care and team personalities. Through these experiences, I realized the importance of creating and sustaining a healthy work environment where everyone's contribution is valued and celebrated. Looking back, I would recommend that a younger self feel more confident and assertive in voicing concerns when something seems wrong with the patient or environment. If I had to do it over again, I would still choose this path and be a nurse, but I would incorporate more evidence-based wellness strategies to mend myself and our broken system.

Two tools have helped me prioritize my professional nursing goals in relation to wellness and focusing my energies on high-priority items that are important to me and impactful to the profession. See Tables 1 and 2 on the following pages.

SETTING GOALS: 5 KEY AREAS OF WELLNESS

TOPIC	SELECTION OF ANNUAL GOALS
Career	☐ Do something each day at work that uses my strengths. ☐ Find a colleague who shares my passion for the nursing profession. ☐ Read a book by a nurse leader who provides insight into their leadership journey.
Community	☐ Volunteer for a cause or event that connects me to my values. ☐ Become a member of one of my professional nursing organizations. ☐ Spend time with a community of like-minded people, like a national nursing conference.
Financial	☐ Make an annual financial plan and track my goals monthly. ☐ Budget earnings for new experiences such as travel and adventure trips. ☐ Raise funds for a medical mission trip that aligns with my goals.
Physical	☐ Track daily walks and the number of steps. ☐ Keep a water bottle nearby and drink plenty of water during the day. ☐ Plan time on my calendar to exercise at least thirty minutes twice a week.
Social	☐ Connect with people who provide a fresh perspective and lift my mood. ☐ Sign up for a networking event that helps me meet like-minded people. ☐ Seek out opportunities within my unit and hospital that will help me connect to my colleagues outside of work.

Table 1

Matrix Map of Prioritizing Goals

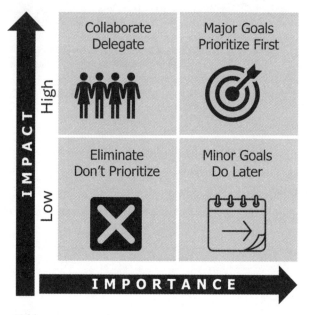

Table 2

When I honor my goals, I am more attuned to my vision of nursing and why I chose this profession. Inventory your wellness goals annually and identify what is most important for your well-being. By writing your goals, you are more likely to achieve them and feel better aligned with your professional calling.

Chapter 16

Taking Care of YOU

Anne Llewellyn

There is a saying I have heard that resonates deeply with me: "If you do not make time for your wellness, you will be forced to make time for your illness." As nurses, we know this is true—but do we care for ourselves? According to experts, the answer is often no. In this section, I aim to explore health and wellness for all, but specifically for nurses, who serve as the backbone of the healthcare system.

Some Known Facts

According to Peterson–KFF,[1] life expectancy has dropped across all race and ethnicity groups in the United States since the onset of the pandemic. For people of color, the decline was more significant. Since 2019, the decline in life expectancy for Black and Hispanic people is four or more years; for Caucasians, the impact is 2.4 years. COVID-19 contributed to excess mortality in 2022 and is on track to be the third-leading cause of death in the US for the third consecutive year.

The American Nation's Nurses Survey Series[2] reveals a tenuous nursing profession. The numbers show that bullying, incivility, and violence are prolific; the emotional health of nurses is still at unhealthy levels; and feelings of stress, frustration, and exhaustion are still elevated two years after the onset of the pandemic. The numbers also reveal that positive feelings, which lead to commitment and performance, have stagnated. Nurses report practicing in workplaces without the necessary number of registered nurse (RN) staff with the right knowledge and skills, and almost half of survey respondents are planning to leave or considering leaving direct patient care.

Post-Pandemic

As we emerge from the pandemic, we have seen new challenges for the well-being of nurses. But with the challenge has come an increase in awareness of nurses' well-being and the need to address the systems, structures, and policies that create workplace vulnerabilities and stressors leading to burnout, fatigue, and poor physical and mental health.

Nurses need help with their purpose, role, function, and the value they bring to the organizations and the patients for whom they provide care. We continue to hear mention of burnout, compassion fatigue, stress, and frustration with the "system," as healthcare professionals' major challenges.

According to the World Health Organization (WHO),[3] burnout is caused by unmanaged, chronic workplace stress. It can occur in any job or sector and results in the following symptoms:

- Mental and physical exhaustion
- Mental distance from the job
- Cynicism about the job

- Reduced effectiveness in the workplace

It's clear that burnout is common in nursing. Nurses work twelve-hour shifts, then pick up more shifts due to insufficient staffing. As a result, they are left both physically and emotionally depleted. They are working with sicker patients with fewer resources to meet those patients' needs. This leads to stress, frustration, and feelings of failure. Nurses often face life-or-death consequences for patients, significantly adding to workplace stress.

According to research on the nursing profession conducted by Zippia,[4] an online recruitment service:

- 95 percent of nurses have felt burnt out within the past three years.
- Only 15.6 percent of nurses felt burnt out in 2019, but since the start of the COVID-19 pandemic, that number has risen to 62 percent.
- Up to 30 percent of all US nurses quit their jobs in 2021.
- 27 percent of nurses who quit have cited burnout as their main reason.
- The current annual turnover rate for nurses is 27.1 percent.

Nursing's Role in Ensuring Health and Wellness

First, examine the terminology that defines and impacts our health and wellness.

Health: Health is the condition of being sound in body, mind, or spirit, especially freedom from physical disease or pain.

Wellness: The WHO[5] defines wellness as more than being free from illness; it is a dynamic process of change and growth, ". . . a state of complete physical, mental, and social well-being, and not merely the absence of disease or infirmity."

Well-being: Well-being is the state of being comfortable, healthy, or happy. An overall sense of wellness will not be achieved without having a balance in these key elements:

- Physical. This includes lifestyle choices that affect the functioning of our bodies. What we eat and how active we are will affect our physical well-being.
- Emotional or psychological. This is our ability to cope with everyday life and reflects how we think and feel about ourselves.
- Social. The extent to which we feel a sense of belonging and social inclusion. How we communicate with others, our relationships, values, beliefs, lifestyles, and traditions are all key factors of social well-being.
- Spiritual. The ability to experience and integrate meaning and purpose in life. This is achieved through being connected to our inner self, nature, or even a higher power.
- Intellectual. It is important to gain and maintain intellectual wellness as it helps us expand our knowledge and skills to live an enjoyable and successful life.
- Economical. Economic wellness is our ability to meet our basic needs and feel secure.

So, Who Is Responsible for Health and Well-Being?

Nurses play a key role in protecting their own health and well-being, but it is a multifaceted issue that demands collective responsibility from the health system, leadership, and the individual. The onus for addressing our health and well-being rests within each of us. Here are eleven tips you can implement to improve your health and well-being:

1. Sleep: take the time to get the rest you need to recharge yourself.
2. Eat a balanced diet: if you don't know how to do this, do an online search or reach out to a nutritionist.
3. Learn to deal with stress.
4. Exercise daily: think about what you like to do—swim, walk, run, exercise at home or in a gym. The activity should help to address the stress in your life.
5. Avoid smoking and alcohol.
6. Be social: make time to meet with family and friends who bring you joy.
7. Find and practice hobbies that bring you joy and purpose.
8. Learn to live in the present: make peace with the past and let the future come to you.
9. Laugh and enjoy the simple things.
10. Engage in improving your work environment: use your voice to address toxic issues impacting your organization for all.
11. If your job makes you unhappy, explore new opportunities: nurses have so many skills that allow them to fit into new roles—so keep your eyes and ears open!

Before he passed, Steve Jobs[6] wrote his farewell. We know him as a successful business executive and entrepreneur—someone who had it all. The line that impacted me the most was this: "Treasure love for your family, love for your spouse, love for your friends . . . Treat yourself well. Cherish others."

We all know that life is short and can change on a dime. Take care of yourself!

Chapter 17

Fostering Sustainable Resilience in Nursing Leadership and Practice through Well-Being as a Strategy

Ian Saludares

Prioritizing the health and well-being of nurse leaders and healthcare workers is more than a preference; it is an essential strategic imperative for the long-term sustainability and success of the nursing profession and the broader healthcare ecosystem. Given the nature of nursing, it becomes mission critical to adopt an approach that prioritizes the well-being of those who dedicate their lives to exceptional patient care.

Promoting Personal Resilience

Whether in leadership positions or at patients' bedsides, nurses operate within a charged, demanding, and intellectually stimulating environment. The unrelenting pressure to deliver top-notch care while juggling responsibilities and making critical decisions can lead to exhaustion and burnout. Nurses are empowered with stress management tools, resilience-building techniques, and effective coping strategies by integrating practices that enhance health and well-being. When nurse leaders prioritize their well-being, it sends a message to their teams that self-care is not only permissible but also indispensable for providing excellent caregiving.

Preserving Experience and Expertise

Experienced nurses bring value to any healthcare institution. Their wealth of knowledge, ability, and honed intuition acquired through years of practice are invaluable assets. However, even dedicated nurses can succumb to the demands placed upon them by their profession. Integrating health and wellness programs creates a safety net that prevents experienced nurses from leaving the profession. When nurses feel appreciated and supported and have access to resources that promote their well-being, they are more likely to stay engaged and committed. This ensures that their ability continues to help patients and the healthcare system.

Encouraging Flexibility and Innovation

Healthcare constantly evolves, with treatments, technologies, and approaches emerging regularly. Nurses at the forefront of patient care must be adaptable and open to change. However, their ability to adapt depends on how they manage stress and overcome challenges. By integrating health and wellness practices into their routines, nurses acquire the emotional agility needed to embrace change, develop skills, and contribute to innovative solutions. When nurse leaders foster an environment encouraging curiosity, experimentation, and continuous learning, they create a workforce more flexible and open to innovation.

Attracting the Next Generation

The shortage of nurses is a widespread concern impacting all areas of healthcare. The younger generation of nurses considers not only the rewards but also the overall quality of life offered by the profession. Integrating health and wellness initiatives into nursing leadership and practice demonstrates the profession's dedication to its practitioners' overall well-being. By showcasing a nurturing work environment that prioritizes a work-life balance, mental health support, and professional growth opportunities, nurse leaders can attract a group of enthusiastic individuals to join the nursing profession.

Promoting Ethical and Patient-Centered Care

Nurses are driven by their dedication to their patients. However, it becomes challenging to provide care when personal well-being is compromised. Nurse burnout can lead to errors, lapses in judgment, and an inability to offer the care that patients deserve. By integrating practices focusing on health and well-being, nurses can ensure that they can fulfill their duty to patients. Patients receive care when nurses feel energized, mentally focused, and emotionally connected.

Transforming Organizational Culture

Blending health and well-being necessitates a transformation of culture. Nursing leaders play a role in facilitating this change by advocating for policies that promote work-life balance, provide health resources, and offer opportunities for professional development. Nurse leaders can also create spaces for dialogue about the challenges nurses face and potential solutions. When healthcare institutions place importance on the well-being of their staff, it fosters an environment that values and supports everyone. This approach promotes cooperation rather than rivalry among colleagues.

Creating Impact across the System

While orchestrating this mix is an undertaking, its influence extends beyond individual healthcare institutions. Nursing leaders can collaborate with policymakers, organizations, and educational institutions to advocate for changes. This may involve advocating for staffing ratios, promoting health resources as standard practice, and assimilating well-being education into nursing curricula. By driving these changes, nurse leaders can ensure that the principles of health and well-being are deeply embedded in the fabric of the healthcare ecosystem.

Collaboration for Sustainable Transformation

Nursing leaders cannot do it alone; sustainable transformation requires an effort from stakeholders. By partnering with human resources departments to develop programs that address physical health, mental health, and work-life balance, success is assured. These programs could include wellness check-ins, access to counseling services, and wellness challenges to promote good habits.

Moreover, fostering collaboration between nurse leaders and frontline staff is crucial. Nurse leaders should establish platforms where staff members can openly express their concerns, propose improvement ideas, and actively take part in shaping a culture that prioritizes well-being. This feeling of involvement not only empowers nurses but also fosters a sense of ownership to create a healthy work environment.

Utilizing Technology for Well-Being

In today's era, technology supports the well-being of nurse leaders and healthcare professionals. Utilizing telehealth platforms, nurse leaders can provide access to health resources and counseling services. Mobile applications can supply techniques to reduce stress, mindfulness exercises, and even virtual support groups where nurses can connect and share their experiences. The use of data analytics to identify patterns of burnout or increased stress among their teams is a powerful tool. This proactive approach enables intervention, ensuring that nurses receive support before their well-being deteriorates.

Sustainable Well-Being for the Future

The interface of health and well-being within nursing leadership and practice will continue evolving. The concept of well-being should be seen as an ongoing effort that adapts to the changing needs of nurses and the ever-evolving healthcare environment. In the future, we may see the integration of artificial intelligence–driven tools that use predictive analytics to show when individual nurses are at risk for stress or burnout based on their work patterns and personal data. This would enable nurse leaders to intervene before burnout takes hold. With a growing focus on promoting diversity, equity, and inclusion within healthcare institutions, we have the unique opportunity to extend the inclusive environment to the well-being space, ensuring that all nurses' unique needs are considered.

The healthcare industry is bound to meet challenges in the years to come. However, nurses can navigate these obstacles with resilience and determination by prioritizing nurse leaders' and healthcare workers' health and well-being. Integrating health and well-being is not merely a response to issues; it is an investment in the long-term sustainability of our profession.

As nurse leaders, we have a responsibility that goes beyond overseeing operations. We are entrusted with nurturing a profession that profoundly affects the lives of patients, families, and communities. By advocating for a healthy work environment, we have an opportunity to sustain our profession as a symbol of compassion, excellence, and innovation.

This integration has far-reaching effects, from nurses' well-being to patient care outcomes, organizational success, and even shaping the broader landscape of healthcare itself. This is a sound investment in the essence of healthcare practice. It recognizes the nursing profession's nature, its practitioners' importance, and the connection between nurse well-being and the quality of care. Nurse leaders play a key role in advocating for these efforts, setting up an atmosphere that fosters and supports nurses, thus strengthening the nursing field for a prosperous future. Nurse leaders can lead this transformation by creating an environment that promotes professional growth among nurses. By prioritizing the well-being of nurse leaders and healthcare professionals, we pave the way toward a thriving future for nursing and the entire healthcare system.

Chapter 18

The DAISY Foundation's Calls to Action

Bonnie and Mark Barnes

As healthcare emerges from the pandemic, too many nurses—including some who played a paramount role in caring for COVID-19 patients and their families—are reconsidering their decision to be nurses. The pressures of working with reduced staff, distressed financial conditions, and a public that often takes its frustrations with healthcare out on nurses and other team members all contribute to higher levels of burnout, compassion fatigue, and sadly, exodus from the profession. Increasingly, healthcare systems are coming to grips with the fact that a healthy healthcare ecosystem demands a workforce that is positive, engaged, and feels valued. More systems are turning their attention to improving the well-being of nurses and improving the environment in which they work.

Our Story

In 1999, our family experienced nursing at its best—clinical excellence combined with extraordinary compassion and sensitivity to our thirty-three-year-old son, Patrick, and our family. When Patrick died after eight weeks in the hospital, we felt compelled to express our gratitude to nurses for all we had experienced. We believed that other patients and families would also want to share their stories of exceptional care. So, we created a means for them to do so by creating the DAISY Award® for Extraordinary Nurses. See Figure 1.

Figure 1

In the early years of our program, cold-calling nursing offices around the United States, offering to partner with them to celebrate their nurses, produced a frequent reply, "Our nurses don't need recognition for doing their jobs." Nurses who were honored by early adopters of the DAISY Award were clearly shocked, overwhelmed with delight, and proud to be recognized. However, often they responded to their award with, "I didn't do anything special. I was just doing my job." Sadly, this response is often heard from honorees today. They do not realize that the seemingly trivial things they do, in addition to the lifesaving strategies they employ, make a profound difference in the experience of those they serve. Nurses care for patients with their brains and with their hearts. These heart-centered acts of kindness are often taken for granted by nurses; yet patients will never forget them. It is those acts of compassion combined with clinical excellence that separate nursing from other healthcare professions. The DAISY Award helps nurses understand that their unique balance of science and art indeed makes them special to the patients and family members in their care.

Meaningful Recognition

The recently embraced focus on nurses' well-being because of the pandemic has brought to light the increased importance of meaningful recognition like the DAISY Award. See Figure 2.

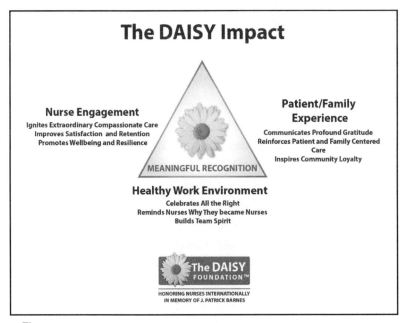

Figure 2

Meaningful recognition is one of the six standards of a healthy work environment (HWE) per research of the American Association of Critical-Care Nurses (AACN).[1] Initially published in 2005, the AACN research has repeatedly been validated over time. Ensuring all six standards are in place has been shown to be vital to nurse retention and more. Contributing to a healthy, positive work environment, DAISY's mission of gratitude and recognition shines a light on all that is right in healthcare organizations. We are committed to helping turn a darkly negative time for healthcare to a more positive one in which nurses are consistently reminded of their purpose in being nurses, and they are regularly reminded of the difference they make to patients and families.

As of 2023, more than 6,000 healthcare facilities and nursing schools internationally are committed to providing meaningful recognition of nurses' contributions by honoring them with the DAISY Award. Over 210,000 nurses have received the award, which honors nurses wherever they practice, wherever they are in their careers. Most importantly, more than 2.5 million times, a patient, family member, or colleague has taken the time to express their gratitude to a nurse by nominating them for DAISY recognition and sharing their story of extraordinary compassionate care.

DAISY nominations describe relationships between patients, families, and nurses—powerful interactions that happen every minute of the day throughout our healthcare systems. Research indicates that patients and families are eager to share their gratitude and that nominating their nurses impacts not only the nurses themselves but also the people writing the nominations. The act of nominating is a "therapeutic reflection," giving a patient or family member a means of balancing their relationship with a nurse who gave so much to them during their experience together. Being able to express gratitude to their nurse through a structured program like the DAISY Award helps bond a patient or family to the organization that cared for them when they were at their most vulnerable.

The pandemic has ebbed, and healthcare is enduring a major redesign of care delivery, leadership structures, and technological enhancements. We at DAISY offer three calls to action related to nurses' well-being.

A Call to Action for Nurses

We call on nurses to reflect on what your care means to patients and families, and to stop saying "I didn't do anything special!" You may not see it as special because you care for patients with expertise and compassion every day. You may take what you do every day for granted. But telling a patient or family member that it wasn't special denies them the positive feeling they get in telling you how you have impacted their lives. We know from our family's experience and from the literature that expressing gratitude to nurses is part of patients' healing process that nurses would never want to minimize.

A Call to Action for the Public

The public's trust in nursing is evidenced in nurses' year-after-year ranking as the most trusted professionals, per Gallup.[2] However, we suspect that the public has no idea how much their appreciation of nurses means to nurses and contributes to nurses' well-being. Therefore, we at DAISY encourage healthcare leaders to reach out to the public. Add to your employees' well-being arsenal with a call to the public to demonstrate their appreciation of the nursing profession's extraordinary contributions to our society. For too long, the public has seen images of beleaguered, exhausted nurses who are worn out caring for patients in the worst conditions. Publicly sharing DAISY

Award nomination stories that are exemplars of nurses' excellence and compassion is one way healthcare organizations can show their communities the powerful impact nurses have and help change the narrative around nursing to the positive. Encouraging the public to show respect and gratitude to nurses will, in turn, enhance the degree to which nurses feel valued and appreciated, crucial factors in their decision to remain in nursing.

Finally, a Call to Action for Compassionate Care

When we started the DAISY Award to honor nurses for their compassionate care, compassion was considered a "soft skill." We were told by some that nurses applied their extensive education, knowledge, and brainpower to clinical treatment of patients and that calling out their acts of kindness was not supportive of the professionalism of nursing. Over the years, increased research has revealed the imperative of compassion in healthcare. The book *Compassionomics* by Stephen Trzeciak and Anthony Mazzarelli[3] describes the tremendous science underpinning how much compassion matters in caring for patients. Delivering clinical excellence in the absence of a human touch is not considered clinical excellence in the minds of patients and families. We at DAISY continue to drive the importance and visibility of compassion as revealed in the award nominations' descriptions of what patients truly value in their healthcare experience. It is more than the successful insertion of an IV into the arm of a frightened child. It's also about the nurse's singing songs from *Frozen* to distract and engage the young patient, making the child more comfortable. It is more than helping a woman deliver her baby successfully when the newborn's grandfather lies terminally ill in the same hospital. It's also about getting a team together to bring the new mom and baby to the grandfather's room so he can hold the baby one time before he dies. It is so much more than educating a patient on what it will be like to live with an ostomy bag. It's also about doing so while sitting by the patient's side, holding his hand, answering his many questions with patience and presence, and helping him know that his life will go on. "Soft skills?" There is nothing soft about combining clinical excellence and patient advocacy with compassion, sensitivity, and kindness.

DAISY began in 1999 as a way for our family to say thank you to nurses for the care Patrick and we experienced during his hospitalization. As a grieving family, filling the hole in our hearts left by Patrick's death with our gratitude to nurses helped us cope with our loss. Today, as the DAISY Award drives meaningful recognition of nurses around the globe, DAISY stands for elevating the importance and value of nurses' extraordinary skills and compassionate care, making their contributions visible to organizations, engaging the public in changing the narrative around healthcare to the positive, celebrating the important and healing impact of the "little things" nurses do for patients and families, and encouraging nurses to accept with grace the gratitude of those they serve. All this contributes to the improved well-being of the largest sector of the healthcare workforce, nurses. While we may not have started DAISY to do all this, we are passionate that DAISY continues to serve as a vehicle to ensure nurses have the life of well-being they deserve, fueled by every ounce of gratitude and respect that the public, their leaders, and their colleagues can give them.

Thank you for answering our calls to action.

Part Three

Wisdom

The nursing workforce is posed to face diverse challenges in the coming decade, including addressing the needs of an aging population with complex medical requirements, meeting the demand for expanded primary care capacity, and integrating healthcare with social determinants of health. Wisdom serves as a framework for translating practice and education into tangible outcomes. Rooted in perspectives, values, and actions, we draw on the resources of nurse leaders who have contributed to our past and present, and who will shape our future.

In the words of Florence Nightingale, "Let us never consider ourselves finished, nurses. We must be learning all our lives."

Indeed, this sentiment resonates in our ongoing efforts. From building upon a proud past to ensuring a sustainable future, from pioneering and leading new initiatives to influencing policy and beyond, transformative nurse disruptors are driving change. Their wisdom will leave a lasting impact on our profession for generations to come.

Chapter 19

Education . . . the Challenges Facing Nursing

Jacqueline Dunbar-Jacob

Our Greatest Challenge Today

The greatest challenge to nurses today is preparing both students and practicing nurses for the rapidly evolving world of healthcare.

New models of care are being advocated and adopted in the United States and around the world. For example, hospital-in-home (the provision of acute-level care in the home) was launched by the Centers for Medicare & Medicaid Services (CMS) in 2020, although it was originally conceived and tested in the late 1990s.[1] Home-based primary care, once the model of care in the US, is resurging with support from CMS. Telehealth delivery of care, although first introduced in the 1950s, reached significant utilization during the COVID-19 pandemic with the 2020 CARES Act and appears to be continuing in use, although at lower levels.[2]

Just as models and settings of care are evolving, so too is the technology of healthcare. Wearable sensors and other smart monitoring devices, artificial intelligence along with cloud-based electronic health records, and strategies such as big data analytics and machine learning have opened the doors to new ways to support healthcare diagnosis and decision-making, quality improvement, telehealth, and communication, as well as to support operational efficiency.[3]

Ensuring that nurses are adequately prepared to function effectively in dynamic healthcare systems is crucial for retaining them in the professional field. Nurses often cite inadequate preparation for practice as a significant factor influencing their decision to exit the profession. Although factors like work environment, safety, and recognition also play a role, the capacity to apply skills and knowledge adeptly in an evolving setting holds particular significance. The demand for competent nurses remains high. Nurses are needed. The population that uses healthcare most often, older adults, is growing, and the number of people entering the workforce (young adults) is declining. The post-war population boom and the continuing increase in life expectancy, combined with declining fertility rates, have contributed to this population shift. This means more people will need care, and fewer people will be available to provide it.

While the population, settings, and modes of delivery of care are evolving, so too is the knowledge base upon which nurses practice. In 2017, Harvard Medical School noted that "the half-life of medical knowledge is currently about 18–24 months,"[4] with half-life referring to the time it takes for 50 percent of extant knowledge to be replaced by new knowledge. In an environment where knowledge taught to the first-year student may be outdated by the time the student reaches the third year, the educational challenge lies in the ability to keep current as a faculty member and as a practicing nurse, and to teach the student how to refresh their knowledge base as time passes. The university's goal of developing lifelong learners has never been more important.

Are we educating our future nurses and our practicing nurses for the near future? Are they learning to deliver care beyond the hospital and ambulatory setting, to utilize technology and analyze data for improved care delivery, to collaborate on the design of new technologies for clinical care, to care for older adults and their unique needs, to become and remain lifelong learners, to be ready for population- and technology-changing knowledge innovations in the future?

Impact of the Pandemic

Perhaps the most striking change seen in recent years is the adoption of telehealth and other technologies to support healthcare.

The use of technology to improve access and quality is not new. The use of telephones to reduce office visits was described in *The Lancet* in 1879; the telecardiogram was described as early as 1906.[5] Numerous projects have examined the use of telehealth from early times to the COVID-19 pandemic. The onset of the pandemic expanded the use of telehealth in ambulatory care as well as in acute care.[6] Government regulations supported this strategy for improving access during the time of extreme social distancing.

But the growth of telehealth is not the only technology that has grown, particularly since the pandemic. The use of artificial intelligence in decision-making has grown, as has the use of wearable monitors. Indeed, the World Health Organization (WHO) has identified over one hundred innovations likely to affect healthcare, with rapid remote diagnostics as one of the most promising areas.[7] Is nursing keeping pace with awareness and with the ability to utilize data produced by these technologies?

Role of the Nurse Educator in Recruitment, Retention, and Ensuring a Healthy Workforce

Nurse educators must prepare the students of today for the healthcare world of the future and must engage the practicing nurse in continuing education that is future oriented.

Given the current concerns over retention, today's answer might be to create a psychologically and physically safe environment that addresses the mental and physical health of the nurse and provides a grateful milieu. While we need to address these issues, we also need to address the evolving knowledge and structure of healthcare; too much of our education within nursing is focused on the *current* structure and knowledge within healthcare. As educators, we need to help our students look to the future, be they pre-licensure or practicing nurses engaged in continuing learning. To stay in the workforce nurses will require an ability to adapt to (and influence) change, to learn continuously, to engage with others, and to question with an eye toward ongoing quality improvement. The nurse of the future is likely to need strengths in quantitative reasoning, the command of technologies to their fullest, to practice in home and telehealth settings, to collaborate with multiple disciplines, and to adapt to changing knowledge. As educators, we play a crucial role in cultivating these skills in the training of new nurses and in the ongoing education of those already in practice.

The Future of Nurse Engagement in Relation to Education—Advocacy

The future for nursing is bright if nursing keeps pace with healthcare developments. One way we can advocate for nursing is to expose students to evolving trends and through interprofessional education.

With the aging of the population and the concurrent increases in healthcare needs, nursing will continue to be a much-needed discipline.

Assessment, monitoring, patient education, as well as care planning and delivery are likely to remain important to nursing care. However, nurses will need to use technology and the data provided by it in executing these activities. They will need to deliver care over the telephone, virtual platforms, and in the home, as well as in institutional settings. They will need to interact with biomedical engineers, data analysts, informaticists, and eHealth technologies in their day-to-day efforts, as well as the multiple clinical and management personnel that are a part of healthcare. They should have the ability to engage in the design and testing of emerging technologies. As educators, we need to expose students early in their preparation to these disciplines and technologies, just as we expose them to blood pressure cuffs and infusion pumps today.

Words of Wisdom for Next-Generation Nurses

Nursing is one of those professions that brings multiple opportunities for career development and career shifts over time. One of those pathways will match your interests and talents. There is a great need, and jobs are plentiful. Go for it! And choose the educational program that provides you with the skills you need for tomorrow's healthcare.

Chapter 20

Discover Your Passion

Cathy Catrambone

My journey as a global leader in nursing has gifted me with unparalleled opportunities to collaborate with nurses and leaders from around the world and to participate in initiatives addressing global health and nursing. I am passionate about the profession, my potential for influence as a positive change agent, and the leadership and learning opportunities that have unfolded throughout my career. Each of these has created awareness of the value of expanding my thinking. Each opportunity has produced benefits far beyond what was imagined.

In the contemporary landscape, it is essential that nurses, individually and collectively as a profession, nurture wisdom in their scope of practice. Each day the wisdom reflected in the decisions made by nurses has the power to transform lives.

Our Challenge

Nursing is both a passion and a profession. Today's greatest challenge is the unprecedented and drastic drop in the population of nurses and the tremendous pressure that nurses today are experiencing. The rate of nurses leaving the profession, the suicide rate, and the focus on those of us who feel at risk and unsupported are beyond anything the profession has ever experienced.[1, 2]

At this critical point, it's essential to let go of the solutions that were used in the past. We must embrace wisdom gleaned from our respective experiences and discover innovative ways of approaching the workforce, our overall well-being, and our future.

Impact of the Pandemic

The pandemic was a global phenomenon that had far-reaching effects, and nurses, among other health professionals, were placed in situations that were never taught in textbooks. The unimaginable became reality, as nurses grappled with death and dying on a grand scale, making life-and-death decisions, and wrestling with our internal self-doubt and the fear for our own safety and that of others. The entire nursing team experienced trauma collectively, some lost their lives to COVID-19, others experienced burnout, some left the profession entirely, and some appeared from the ashes to shine brighter than ever. Today, nurses bear the burden of post-traumatic stress, impacting their mental and physical well-being as a professional community. We find ourselves in a situation that we had not foreseen.

We've experienced waves of social conflict, injustice, and a surge of violence and depression. Our lack of mental health resources and providers has been exposed to the world. We already knew there was a gap, but now it is front and center, and nursing has been charged with addressing these issues. Incivility and abuse have eroded the profession's retention efforts.

Nursing's Role in Reclaiming the Passion

To reclaim our passion for a noble profession, we must work collectively to appreciate diverse perspectives and embrace emerging technologies in a morally responsible way to foster solutions in these complex circumstances. Recruitment and retention of passionate, healthy, and engaged nurses are significant issues that will affect the future of health systems and educational institutions on a grand scale. Nursing leaders need to inject the passion, zest, and excitement for the possibilities the profession offers, which are endless. It is all about the connections and the relationships built within the profession. Creating environments that are supportive to nurses and genuinely caring about the nurse's well-being can make a difference. Developing mentorship programs for nurses that are new to organizations and systems is a step. Finding ways to foster growth for the nurse is a key to unlocking their potential to be creative and innovative.

Engagement

1. The future of nurse engagement is a dynamic landscape, and it requires the ability to adapt to the ever-shifting work and social context within which nurses work. To navigate this terrain effectively, nurses can draw inspiration from the passion that brought them to the profession. Nursing engagement hinges on our ability to hear and respond to the reality of our colleagues, to meet them where they are, to foster understanding, and to create platforms for novel solutions.

2. A powerful approach to cultivate engagement is creating transparency and participation through shared governance within healthcare systems and organizations. This

allows for collaboration among nurses from diverse backgrounds, both within and outside their organizations. It opens doors to influence legislative changes that will enhance nursing practice, improve access to healthcare, and promote the safe delivery of care.

3. Throughout this journey, nurses must be actively engaged as insightful and effective collaborators across various fronts. This includes taking part in professional organizations, extending involvement beyond the nursing sphere, engaging with community groups, and contributing to local, state, and national initiatives. Ensuring that the voice of the nurse resonates everywhere is crucial. Consequently, organizations play a vital role by creating an environment conducive to nursing.

Reflection

The healthcare environment and the social and professional experience of nurses have changed drastically, and even though the profession has been recognized by the public as trustworthy for years, nurses are experiencing violence and abuse at an alarming rate.[3]

For those considering the profession today, I urge you to think of a story or a moment that made it clear that nursing was the right choice; embrace the passion that you feel when you think about that moment. Be willing to go beyond the borders of one's current beliefs or prior experiences. It's important to know that the nursing profession offers vast opportunities and to reflect on what is most important to one's own, unique identity. In other words, think about how you express your purpose in life through nursing.

My personal learning journey has been continuous, leading me to identify three fundamental concepts that I advise those entering the profession to contemplate. Grasping these concepts at the onset of your career enables you to chart a course that aligns with your individual values. The title of this chapter is at the heart of these thoughts: 1) discover your passion, 2) be intentional about your journey, and 3) put yourself at the table. My interest in Sigma Theta Tau International (Sigma) and the organization's mission for nursing sparked my own growth and have played a significant role in shaping my perspective of global health. I was intentional in selecting the steps that would result in a progressive leadership journey within the organization. Starting at the local level, I moved to regional, and then, in 2015, was elected to serve as president. Per the mission of developing nurse leaders anywhere to improve healthcare everywhere, it was an honor to be at the table with nurse leaders from around the world to address issues facing nursing and healthcare. This is our collective passion!

Chapter 21

Be Intentional

Melissa Burdi

Do you find yourself frustrated following the same routine day in and day out, wishing for a different outcome or result? Perhaps that result means increased workflow efficiency, greater work-life balance, or improved on-the-job satisfaction. If this sounds like you, then it's possible you have encountered burnout at some point in your career.

According to the American Nurses Association (ANA),[1] the nursing profession saw a mass exodus during the pandemic due to burnout. Work conditions were unfavorable prior to 2020 and were further worsened by the unprecedented challenges experienced during the pandemic. Post-pandemic, new obstacles have surfaced, placing additional strains on the healthcare system. These challenges include a disengaged workforce and the accelerated integration of digital infrastructure, affecting the effectiveness and efficiency of nurses' workflows. Moreover, these factors played a role in economic instability, impacting the long-term viability of healthcare organizations.

Crisis Mode

Why is this? Simply put: We are in crisis mode. Nurses are the largest part of the healthcare workforce,[2] and the demand for nursing expertise outweighs the current supply. Complexity of care, influenced by economic and political forces, has strained the healthcare system, and nurses have experienced poor working conditions with a lack of focus on self-care. We urgently require a fresh infusion of ideas to rectify the shortcomings in our delivery model, and the time to do this was yesterday.

The Challenge

The trillion-dollar question remains: How do we fix this? Lead with intent. Change starts from within. Knowing our strengths, we can use our capabilities as individuals and as healthcare teams. When nurses are equipped with knowledge and skills such as leadership and business acumen, they can negotiate fair conditions of employment and advocate for work-life balance. Healthcare organizations, academic institutions, and nurse leaders across all settings must partner to re-engage nurses, actively listen, and identify opportunities for improvement. Caring for and retaining our skilled workforce remains one of the biggest obstacles our nursing profession faces today.

The already exorbitant economics of healthcare were agitated by COVID-19, with annual spend approaching nearly one-fifth of the gross domestic product (GDP) in the US. According to the Centers for Medicare & Medicaid Services (CMS), total health expenditure has grown since the pandemic and is predicted to surpass average rates of growth for the GDP over the next eight years.[3] Societal habits, fueled by a desire for instant gratification and extravagant spending, contrast sharply with the sluggish pace at which investments have been directed toward resolving bottlenecks in the healthcare infrastructure. The pandemic underscored this disparity vividly.

Prior to the pandemic, many groundbreaking advancements were on the horizon, including the inception of virtual reality (VR) and artificial intelligence (AI). The pandemic served as a catalyst, catapulting technological advancements forward out of sheer need. As a result, procedures evolved. The human touch took on new meaning. Our virtual presence through telehealth expanded. Nurses on the front line were deemed essential workers who reported to work to care for the gravely ill. The growing number of people who fell ill to COVID-19 outpaced our ability to respond. Academia was tasked with producing more entry-level nurses than ever before, and the healthcare environment as we knew it mirrored battle zones at best.

While nurses fell ill themselves, their perseverance and resolve never wavered. Since the onset of the pandemic, nursing has consistently retained its status as the most trusted profession. For over two decades, nurses, more than any other profession, have been uniquely positioned to influence healthcare in a safe and compassionate way.[4]

As nurses demonstrated resilience, they emerged as a beacon of hope and catalysts for change. Global awareness surrounding social determinants of health and health disparities were brought to the forefront during the pandemic, and the voice of nurses quickly gained traction. The power of nurses in numbers was leveraged, which influenced important discussion at the legislative level. Three key priorities aimed at reducing nurse burnout garnered overdue attention: creating a safer work environment, improving the nursing pipeline, and achieving safe staffing ratios. In 2023, the ANA took bold steps to introduce legislation to close these gaps. Colossal changes with intentionality are needed now, and we cannot afford to continue with the "wait and see" approach.[5]

Recruitment and retention of a thriving workforce continues to be top of mind for nurse leaders. New models of care that replace antiquated ways of operating are essential. Design thinking is needed, and leaders at the bedside and in the boardroom must collaborate to create new and improved workflows. According to the United States Bureau of Labor Statistics,[6] the nursing workforce is expected to grow by 6 percent over the next decade, from 3.1 million to 3.3 million registered nurses (RNs) by the year 2031, an increase of nearly 200,000. Sadly, this growth does not meet the demand needed to sustain the future of healthcare.

Long work hours, inflexible scheduling, increased staffing ratios, and lack of value in the workplace all contribute to low morale and threaten the ability to recruit new nurses. Having a nursing shortage not only contributes to burnout but also burdens the overall healthcare system. Hospitals are taxed in their ability to provide safe and high-quality care; health outcomes, including increased morbidity and mortality, remain at risk.

Our Future

What can we expect for the future? High turnover and nurse fatigue will persist, and nurse retention will continue to be challenged by outside competition willing to compensate nurses by more than two to three times the average salary. If we do not optimize now, we will see more of the same versus anything different.

As nurse leaders, we have an ethical obligation to act with beneficence as we re-envision a new and improved nursing workforce with outside-the-box thinking. A change in basic assumptions in how we approach education is needed. Academic institutions must collaborate with clinical partners to respond to changing healthcare needs. More experts are needed on the front line with continuous upskilling and reskilling. Creative alternatives to engage and retain the nursing workforce—including on- and off-ramps that support those pursuing and leaving the nursing profession—are imperative. Options are attractive for employees, and retention is key for employers. Are you ready to be part of the change?

Engagement

As we ponder how to improve nurse engagement for the future, we must begin by identifying the current shortcomings. While patients are the voice of the customer, nurses are the largest voice of the US healthcare system. Purposeful connection between leaders and nurses at the point of care is needed to generate positive engagement in the workplace. With intentionality and neuroplasticity, it is possible to reframe our thinking to foster higher levels of engagement. How do we do this?

1. Be deliberate. Focus on individual development. Create succession plans that support the future. Team engagement does not happen on autopilot.
2. Seek to listen before you speak. The order in which we do things matters to those we lead.
3. Cause and effect are real. Keep your fingers on the pulse to foster retention and team cohesiveness.
4. Leaders have an obligation to invest in the workforce of tomorrow.
5. Adopt and promote the three Es: Empowerment, Education, and Energy.
6. Collaborate with professional boards and organizations to elevate the autonomy and authority of nurses.
7. Don't boil the ocean. Be laser focused on your goals and invite your team to provide input so that everyone has a stake in the game.

8. Reflection is a powerful tool to have in your arsenal. Wisdom, when passed on in the form of professional mentorship, can also be extremely impactful.

Reflections for My Younger Self

Today, I subscribe to what I call Pearls of Wisdom; they are my guiding principles (see below) that I would share with my younger self.

Pearls of Wisdom

- Always assume positive intent in others. Relationships are your greatest asset.
- Approach life with a growth mindset.
- Take care of yourself and keep your cup full. Your physical and mental health is key to your longevity.
- Be confident. Never underestimate what you bring to the table. Confidence plus humility is the best prescription for success.
- Take calculated risks and don't be afraid to fail. It's guaranteed we won't get things right every time. Live curiously and remember innovation requires persistence.
- Set boundaries. These can only be determined by you, and you know yourself best.
- While strengths can be cultivated, most are innate. Be the authentic leader that YOU are and leverage your strengths. Capitalize where you excel, not where you are deficient.

- Embrace resilience. Setbacks happen. The challenge and pressures that nurses face in healthcare are real.
- Dare to be different.
- To know oneself is to love oneself. Be comfortable in your own skin.
- Learn how to read a room.
- Realize that a mistake is only a mistake when we push the replay button repeatedly and choose not to learn from it.
- There is no separation between person and profession. We are one. Be the person you want to be every day and center your priorities around what matters to you most. Remember that we all have different goals, and that is OK.
- Act with integrity and be brave. Have the courage to step forward when other step back. Our nursing profession needs leaders like you.

Pace e Bene

Chapter 22

Voice and Power

Kathleen Bartholomew

The greatest challenge facing nursing today is myopic embedding—from national leaders to frontline staff, we are focused on putting out fires and not on their cause. For example, vast amounts of time, energy, and resources are being poured into retention and recruitment initiatives. Nursing leaders diligently pursue innovative programs and new personnel configurations to retain nurses with limited budgets. We are wasting a tremendous amount of time. If we can shift perception, we can reclaim our power.

A root cause analysis of the key issues nurses face reveals that our challenges are caused by the structure itself. Nurses work in a system designed to maximize profits for their shareholders—whether you work in a for-profit or non-profit organization. Dedicated nurses focused on their patients do not realize the conundrum they live in every day: providing skilled care in a system that values profit above caring, healing, and wellness. If we applied the theory that "structure dictates process, which dictates outcomes," then our precious energy would be poured into creating a new structure.

Nurses do, however, perceive the symptoms of our dysfunctional structure: horizontal hostility, inadequate staffing, faculty shortages, moral distress, and burnout. Expanding perception is critical. If we are ever to come together, share our collective wisdom, and address our profession's challenges, we must compassionately widen the lens and address these symptoms with the same knowledge and care that we give to our patients.

Task Saturation

By far the greatest source of stress is task saturation. Time and motion studies have proven that nurses have adapted to an unrealistic number of tasks. Because of human adaptability, incremental changes went unnoticed. By 2017, nurses averaged over 624 tasks in a twelve-hour shift with 40 percent of their time spent multitasking both tasks and communication.[1] The pandemic exacerbated these numbers with the donning of protective gear, staffing shortages, and the absence of family members at the bedside. Working in a constant state of motion alters our biology.

When humans overuse the muscles in our brain responsible for monitoring and performing tasks, the muscles that are designated for paying attention to relationships weaken. We do not notice, or choose not to notice, eye-rolling, sarcasm, blaming, and bickering because these middle-school behaviors sap our energy and distract our focus from the patient. Uncivil behaviors undermine our efforts, rob us of energy, and keep our profession divided and oppressed. As tasks and stress increase, so does horizontal hostility.

Horizontal Hostility

The greatest barrier to addressing horizontal hostility is our collective shame that it exists in the first place. When I began collecting stories from nurses twenty years ago, I was overwhelmed with confusion. "How is it even possible that nurses could experience such mean behaviors from their peers—in a profession based on caring?" The short answer is that horizontal hostility is not about nursing. It is a symptom of powerlessness that happens when any group is dominated by another. Nurses feel this lack of power every day. Healthcare charge nurses and managers do not have a voice or power in adequately staffing their units because the grid is controlled by the budget. A lack of equipment or personnel may cause nurses to use hostile behaviors without realizing they are doing so. When oppressed, humans unconsciously turn on each other because they cannot direct their power upward.

The derogatory impact of hostility is insidious and invisible. Nurses report burnout, lethargy, depression, leaving an organization or department, and even suicidal thoughts because horizontal hostility exists just below our level of cultural awareness.[2] If hostility is the reason a nurse has decided to leave, they will not mention it in their exit interview.[3]

If you say something, then you could become the target or may be perceived as a "troublemaker" or not being a "team player." If you watch hostility happening to others, then you see the consequences and learn to keep quiet. There are strong neurological consequences. Research shows that just watching these behaviors strikes the same emotional cord in the witness as it does in the victim.[4] If you are silent, then shame turns inward, which can make you mentally, emotionally, or physically sick. In a toxic culture where horizontal hostility is tolerated, sick days slowly increase, overburdening the nurses who did show up to work short-staffed—unless we learn best practice for creating a culture of kindness.

Power and Voice

The American Association of Colleges of Nursing (AACN) standards say that "nurses must be as competent in their communication skills as they are in their clinical skills." Communication hardwires trust. What does communication competency look like? The ability to have a professional conversation about anything that concerns you with anyone, including your manager or a physician.

Our words are our power. If we hardwire good habits and create conditions where every member of the team can speak their truth, trust is established, and a culture of kindness flourishes. People value the critical importance of cultivating relationships. Under these ideal conditions, if a nurse has a problem with a peer, they will directly approach that person in private with the goal of compassionately creating a space where they can see eye-to-eye. You would never hear a nurse talking about another nurse who is not present.

Never take these learned behaviors personally. Hostility is a group trauma, and chances are that your peers have similar experiences. Speak up and claim our collective power.

You could say, "I noticed that . . . you rolled your eyes . . . you were sarcastic . . . you ignored me . . ." etc. These words make non-verbal behaviors visible. Finding your own voice in moments when someone has stripped you of your power either verbally or non-verbally is of vital importance to your psychological well-being.

Hierarchies are common in healthcare culture. Physicians have historically held more power than nurses, nurses have more power than nursing assistants, etc. In a hierarchy, everyone knows one another's "place," and the overt and covert behaviors of ignoring, avoiding eye contact, whining, blaming, etc. are unconsciously used to remind people to get back in the cultural line. This is where managers can role-model collegiality. Even though titles and wages differ, we are all equal in value to the patient. A skilled surgeon might flawlessly repair a cervical fracture and then place their patient in a hard collar for protection. But if dietary does not send in the liquid-only tray, the patient will choke. Our roles are cohesive, and our patients will be safe when we create an environment in which everyone feels seen, valued, and free to speak their truth.

Cognitive Dissonance

As our individual voices rise one by one, our power will be unleashed. Collective self-esteem rises, and nursing will be freed from oppression.

In the movie *Barbie*, Gloria passionately describes how her deprogramming technique works: "You just expose and give voice to the cognitive dissonance." Cognitive dissonance is inconsistency in thoughts or attitudes when contradictory beliefs are held at the same time. Because behaviors make no sense, humans push conflicting thoughts out of their realm of awareness just to be able to function. Exposing cognitive dissonance in nursing has the same effect. If we uncover contradictory expectations, nurses can wake up to the power dynamics that keep them oppressed.

Nurses take their responsibility to supply safe, high-quality care seriously. The charge nurse knows exactly how many nurses are needed to staff the shift responsibly, because they have the vital decision-making data: 1) the real-time acuity of the patients, and 2) the skill and experience level of the oncoming shift. We dutifully accept the responsibility to keep our patients safe; yet we lack the power to summon the resources needed to carry out this goal. This is crazy-making cognitive dissonance.

Every nurse at every level has one thing in common: we have all been asked to do more with less—while health systems, executives, and processed food companies reap billions in profits.[5,6]

Another example of dissonance is the mission of our institutions. We are consistently told that the ideal is safe, quality, evidenced-based care. Yet our daily experiences do not always mesh with this mission. If safe, quality care was really the top priority, nurses would have the staff and resources they need to do their jobs. The reality is that our healthcare system is a business that profits on disease and illness.

When an individual or group has no power over an extended period, learned helplessness becomes the norm. This is most clear in nursing's fight for safe staffing. The metaphor used to explain learned helplessness describes how a baby elephant is chained, tries thousands of times to get away, and then eventually gives up. Then the owner removes the chain because he knows the elephant will never try again. Nurses fight for staffing grids and ratios instead of for their own power and ability to make this critical decision. There is no chain.

Hope

Look up! Nurses are the powerful force needed to change the trajectory of disease in America.[7] The oppression and resulting hostility we have experienced comes from the medical for-profit model. As each of us commits to dauntlessly speak our truth, we break the bonds of oppression. Together, we will create a system focused on wellness and prevention where nurses thrive. This revolution begins with the realization that our daily interactions ARE the future of nursing.

Chapter 23

Sixteen Strategic Steps That Drive Wisdom . . . Securing Our Future!

Alina Kushkyan

Our profession imparts valuable lessons through interactions with students and faculty, team members, and global colleagues. Regardless of our location, we encounter many challenges at home and abroad. Nurses are the backbone of the healthcare system, playing a decisive role in delivering health services on both local and global scales. The nursing profession needs constant and consistent development. Our shared objective is to develop qualified nurses who are professionally trained, well-educated, and poised to become wise future leaders. This collective effort will improve the health of people and the quality of their care.

The role of nurses has changed, and responsibilities have increased in intensity. Nurses are aware of the need for an integrated approach to education and care. Lifelong learning mandates a focus on knowledge and wisdom. This begins with education and critical thinking aimed at improving knowledge in information technologies, public health, epidemiology, infectious diseases, psychology, and leadership.

Today's nurses have seen changes in how information is used, the need to cope with disaster preparation, and more. Today's nurses must have good clinical experience and sound judgment combined with an understanding of human nature and life's complexities. This involves the ability to discern between right and wrong, to view situations from multiple perspectives, and to apply accumulated knowledge in a compassionate and empathetic way. Wise individuals have the rare ability to find balance and harmony amid the chaos of life, making them invaluable mentors, leaders, and friends.

Wisdom

Wisdom holds great significance in both personal and societal contexts. On an individual level, wisdom fosters emotional resilience, self-awareness, and the ability to adapt to life's challenges. It helps nurses make informed decisions, fostering a sense of purpose and contentment. In society, nurse leaders guide with integrity, promoting the well-being of their communities and inspiring others to follow paths of righteousness and kindness. In the journey of life, wisdom is a beacon that illuminates our path, guiding us toward better decisions and a profound understanding of the world around us. It is a virtue worth pursuing, for it enriches our lives and the lives of those around us. By cultivating a curious mind, practicing mindfulness, and embracing empathy, we can nurture the seeds of wisdom within us and watch them blossom into a life of purpose, compassion, and fulfillment.

A Multifaceted Approach

The pandemic brought dramatic changes in the workforce and workplace, making us acutely aware of the need for well-being. As leaders, we are challenged to keep adequate staffing. Addressing recruitment, retention, and the cultivation of a healthy workplace involves a multi-faceted approach. Here are some strategies wise leaders can consider:

1. Competitive Compensation: Competitive salaries and benefits are crucial for attracting and retaining talented employees. It shows your commitment to valuing their contributions and ensuring their financial well-being.

2. Healthy Working Conditions: Providing a safe, clean, and comfortable work environment is essential. Focus on ergonomics, proper ventilation, and equipment maintenance to enhance employee well-being and productivity.

3. Work-Life Balance: Promote work-life balance by encouraging flexible working arrangements, such as remote work and flexible hours. This helps reduce burnout and improves employee morale.

4. Health and Wellness Programs: Implement initiatives that promote physical, mental, and emotional well-being. This could include fitness programs, stress management workshops, and access to mental health resources.

5. Healthy Food Options: Offer nutritious food options in the workplace, whether through cafeteria choices or vending machines. A well-balanced diet contributes to employee health and energy levels.

6. Government Support: Advocate for policies that support employee well-being, such as healthcare coverage, family leave, and mental health support. Collaborating with government initiatives can create a supportive ecosystem.

7. Professional Development: Invest in your team to enhance their skills; this proves your commitment to their growth.

8. Inclusive and Diverse Culture: Create an inclusive workplace that values diversity—an environment where everyone feels respected and valued contributes to a positive work atmosphere.

9. Transparent Communication: Keep employees informed about organizational goals, decisions, and changes. Transparent communication builds trust and helps employees feel more engaged.

10. Recognition and Feedback: Recognize and appreciate employee contributions regularly. Constructive feedback helps employees improve and grow professionally.

11. Leadership Development: Train and nurture strong leaders within the organization who can effectively manage teams, communicate goals, and support their employees.

12. Employee Involvement: Involve employees in decision-making processes that affect their work. This gives them a sense of ownership and empowerment.

13. Sustainability Initiatives: Implement environmentally friendly practices that align with the values of modern workers who prioritize sustainability.

14. Education Support: Offer opportunities for continued education and skill development. This could include supporting employees pursuing higher education or attending workshops and conferences.

15. Performance Recognition: Implement fair and transparent performance evaluation processes that reward excellence and supply growth opportunities.

16. Community Engagement: Encourage employees to engage in community service and social-impact initiatives. This contributes to a sense of purpose and connection. Creating a healthy workplace requires ongoing commitment and a willingness to adapt as the needs of the workforce evolve.

Wisdom . . . Ongoing

Wisdom requires us to recognize the importance of integrating technical expertise with holistic patient care and ethical decision-making. As a dean, I see a focus on holistic care and wise nurses who understand patients' emotional, psychological, and social needs in addition to their medical condition. Ethical decision-making is imperative; nurses will need to apply wisdom to navigate perilous situations, balancing medical advancements with ethical considerations. At the core of wisdom is continuous learning. As our healthcare landscape rapidly evolves, it will be critical to require nurses to continuously update their knowledge and skills if we are to maintain the stability of a skilled workforce. Nurse engagement will evolve from interdisciplinary collaboration, allowing nurses to glean valuable insights into practice and outcomes. Cultural competence will drive nurses to provide culturally sensitive care that respects patients' individuality. Emotional intelligence, the new wisdom, will allow nurses to connect with patients on a deeper level, develop effective communication skills, and build trusting relationships.

We now understand the value of a healthy work environment, one that promotes well-being and prevents burnout. Wise nurses will prioritize self-care and recognize when they need to seek support to maintain their mental and emotional health. Wise nurses will take on leadership roles and advocate for patient rights, safe working conditions, and improved healthcare policies. Their wisdom will influence positive change within healthcare systems. Research and innovation will drive changes, and wise nurses will play a key role in developing innovations that transform practice and outcomes.

Wisdom is a key factor in engagement. By embracing wisdom, nurses can navigate the complexities of the healthcare landscape, contribute to positive changes, and continue to supply compassionate, patient-centered care.

I have been a dean and physician throughout my career; I have founded a nursing school and have fostered opportunities for nurses to advance their education and practice. I would tell a younger version of myself, if I were considering the profession, to be brave, learn, improve, develop, and make an invaluable contribution to the healthcare space by promoting a healthy lifestyle. Integrate within the global nursing community and contribute to nursing wisdom locally and globally. Conduct research and joyfully commit to this profession to change the world for the better through kindness, mercy, compassion, professionalism, leadership, global cooperation, and of course wisdom!

Reflection

The pandemic has changed the world of healthcare. The healthcare system was marked by unpreparedness, insufficient equipment, insufficient knowledge, and a lack of wisdom and applicable skills. We now know that we need a newfound respect for the role of medical workers and the ability to respond to emergencies in real time. The realization that one must learn to improve throughout life, accumulate experience, practice, and embrace global training standards and technologically innovative approaches to the training of nurses will drive our future. Our goal is to prepare next-generation nurses. One piece of wisdom gleaned from the pandemic is that no person, organization, or country can change anything for the better without global cooperation. Integration and global partnerships are critical to our success during crisis events. The pandemic highlighted the importance of robust public health systems and international collaboration focusing on early detection and rapid response.

Who will succeed us? A new generation of nurses who work with complex equipment and who have the wisdom, knowledge, and ability to plan, analyze, and take responsibility for their activities will succeed us. This is our mandate to humanity—to attach importance to the health of each individual and to our respective systems.

Chapter 24

Unleashing the Power of Nurses . . . Transforming Healthcare

Kim Evans

The Challenges

Two of the greatest challenges facing nurses today are role ambiguity and role conflict. Nurses are educated to assess the whole person—body, mind, and spirit—and to focus on wellness and disease prevention. Yet in many nursing positions, nurses are forced to practice in a medical model that predominantly addresses physical issues and focuses on sick care. Even though nurses are aware of the critical significance that emotional/psychological and spiritual aspects play in one's health, the current organizational structure is not designed to meet these patient needs.[1] This creates role conflict.

The Conflict

When an organization's mission statements include "patient-centered care," yet units are not staffed appropriately based on acuity, or when office visits are limited to fifteen minutes, role ambiguity results. Nurses and nurse practitioners (NPs) feel frustrated, depressed, and powerless, knowing there are more effective ways to deliver care that would truly transform the health of individuals and communities. We innately know that an ounce of prevention is worth a pound of cure, yet our healthcare system is reactive rather than proactive, thriving on disease care and waiting until one gets sick, *then* trying to fix it. We are left with a big hole in our nursing soul.

This role conflict and ambiguity became the impetus I needed to leave my position as a critical care clinical nurse specialist (CNS) and start my own integrative medicine clinic. Finally, I could practice holistically, as I was trained.

The pandemic certainly heightened the realization of the brokenness of our disease-care system. Those with comorbidities and chronic illnesses were found to be more susceptible to COVID-19 and later died.[2] Laires et al. found a positive correlation between chronic disease and the contraction and severity of COVID-19. In my practice, I was amazed that throughout the entire first year of COVID-19, none of our patients were diagnosed positive. During the second year of the pandemic, while more of our patients did contract COVID-19, none of our patients nor their family members had COVID-19-related deaths . . . I do not believe this is a coincidence. Our focus on wellness and disease prevention includes supporting patients' immune systems, and we adopted protocols to enhance this process.

As healthcare providers, we missed an excellent opportunity during the pandemic. While media attention focused on obtaining a vaccine,[3] there was little to no attention given to creating healthy habits or lifestyle behaviors that could prevent chronic diseases. Since the pandemic, more people are assuming responsibility for their own health, and some are seeking new models of healthcare that will support them in reaching their best health.

Nurses Hold the Solution

Nurses are essential to meeting these needs. Throughout the section on workforce, we heard the numbers—and they are staggering. The question is, Would nurses be quietly quitting if there were alternative models in which to practice? Models that:

- used an integrative approach to healing;
- fostered teamwork valuing each discipline equally;
- encouraged each team member's contribution from their highest level of training;
- promoted a healthy work-life balance allowing care team members to reach their own optimal health while modeling the same for patients; and
- used nurse coaches to help patients in all aspects of their life.

I posit that nurses would return to the workforce in droves.

In my practice, I have seen that intentionally creating a healing environment for patients is as important as any procedure or medication because our mere presence is an intervention. Patients ache to be heard and seen. They want to share the story of their disEASE journey to feel that someone cares about their health.

Testing and objective data matter, but they must be evaluated within the context of each individual person. All aspects of health need to be addressed. For instance, Julia (age thirty) and her husband struggled with infertility for seven years. Both had been through multiple tests and had seen several different providers. She had previously become pregnant but lost the baby at sixteen weeks gestation and was devastated. Further hormonal testing provided a possible solution; we tested for DHEA and testosterone, as well as ApoE, the gene responsible for metabolizing cholesterol. From this panel, I prescribed a supplement to balance her hormones and a nutrition and exercise plan based on her genetic expression. A comprehensive approach to care held the key to her ability to become pregnant and to deliver a beautiful baby girl!

Unleashing Our Power

It is time for us as nurses to step into our power . . . to say NO to disease-care and YES to healthy models of healthcare. Imagine if nurses were encouraged to "think outside the box" and become disruptors of the status quo. Nurses are the solution to creating, developing, and implementing new models of healthcare based on wellness and disease prevention that are both affordable and accessible.

There are numerous examples of nurses who have shifted the paradigm and done just that.

- Candice E., an NP, has been instrumental in transforming the health of citizens in her rural community. Starting with a food pantry, she gradually taught residents to eat healthy by helping them grow an organic garden. She created an assessment tool to determine their underlying social determinants of health and then developed an IT interface platform so their immediate needs could be matched with resources in real time, connecting and strengthening community.
- Carolina J. and Dr. Kenneth A., NPs, created subscription-based vital direct primary care. No insurance is filed, which allows the NPs to practice based on the needs of each patient. They are not constrained by time, specific Medicare measures, billing codes, and excessive

documentation to justify those billing codes. They simply take care of the patient. Both the NPs and the patients are thriving in this model and love it!

- A new model on the forefront is the adapted public utility model, which is led by nurses, and bypasses traditional third-party insurers and addresses the social determinants of health.[4]

Neither American businesses nor individuals can sustain the rising costs of our profit-driven, fee-for-service, upside-down incentivized disease-care system—especially when our national outcomes are dismal. It is time for new paradigms. True value-based care will exist when the focus is placed on quality and outcomes instead of quantity and profit maximization.

Value-based care is better at building long-term relationships with patients—addressing all their needs. Who is better than nurses to do this?

The current dysfunctional disease-care system is ripe for opportunities. Nurses are the key providers to navigate the needed change. There are opportunities to disrupt the status quo and expedite healing healthcare. For example:

- Advocate for full practice authority in EVERY state for all NPs.
- Insist that nursing is represented on every healthcare-related board of directors in the country and volunteer to be on those boards.
- Be a role model and improve your own health.
- Continue to dream and explore how to transform healthcare. We do make a difference!
- Start your own practice.
- Network with nurses who are transforming healthcare.

- Pursue ongoing education, including bachelor's, master's, DNP, MBA, or IT degrees.

Reflection

As I reflect on my own career trajectory and the drivers that caused me to seek change, I am more aware than ever before that role conflict and ambiguity would NOT exist in a nurse-led system. Now is our time to unleash the power of nursing by creating, designing, and implementing new paradigms for healthcare based on wellness and disease prevention!

Chapter 25

A 360-Degree Lens: Connecting the Dots between Workforce, Well-Being, and Wisdom

Christina Dempsey

As a nurse executive, educator, patient, and family member of patients with cancer and traumatic brain injury, I have viewed healthcare with a 360-degree lens. These experiences have offered wisdom, a focus on the healthcare workforce, and the need for nurses and other providers to feel safe. These areas are interconnected—the workforce must feel safe and well for nurses to provide care and experience fulfillment, and wisdom gleaned from our experience helps to drive how we structure work, the processes we deploy, and the outcomes we achieve.

The greatest challenge facing our profession is that people are not able to connect with why they do what they do—they do not feel the joy in the journey. This is multifactorial and starts well before they become healthcare professionals. There is too much to do, not enough people or time to do it, and too much of a focus on how to carry out tasks rather than why it matters and how it connects. Nursing has traditionally been considered the holistic healthcare discipline in that nurses have understood not just the clinical impact of disease processes and health but also the psychosocial, emotional, and community impact. There is such a focus on the technical aspects and tasks that the holistic part of nursing care is getting lost. With that loss, nurses don't find fulfillment in a task-driven, checklist-oriented job. Nurses did not come to work to carry out tasks; they came to make a difference and to help people. This incongruity causes burnout, lack of trust, and lack of hope that trickles down to the patient, who then feels less safe, more alone, and more vulnerable.

Impact of the Pandemic

The pandemic exacerbated these issues, but it did not create them. At the onset of the pandemic, patients and communities saw how hard nurses were working and the sacrifices they were making; they referred to nurses as heroes to be celebrated. However, though nurses and other healthcare professionals are still working hard and making sacrifices, there is less understanding, and workplace violence is on the rise.

The National Council of State Boards of Nursing (NCSBN) unveiled its research, titled "Examining the Impact of the COVID-19 Pandemic on Burnout and Stress Among US Nurses," in a panel titled "Nursing at the Crossroads: A Call to Action." Key findings revealed that approximately 100,000 registered nurses (RNs) left the workforce during the pandemic due to stress, burnout, and retirement, and another 610,388 RNs reported an intent to leave the workforce by 2027.[1] Nursing education can't keep pace with the departures. Because there are fewer nurses, there are fewer faculty and fewer clinical placements for students, thus limiting the number of qualified applicants that can be admitted. Nursing schools turned away over 90,000 qualified applicants to nursing schools last year.[2] Union activity is increasing, and state legislatures are considering mandated nurse-to-patient ratios. Unfortunately, these mandates will result in bed closures and service reduction for patients because nurses are not available. Travel or agency nursing saw an uptick during COVID-19, often with extremely unreasonable prices that wreaked havoc on hospital finances, further reducing their ability to supply services and forcing many rural hospitals to close. Rates and volumes are coming back into line but will likely never be what they were prior to the pandemic.

Safe staffing, innovative care models, shared decision-making, and academic partnerships are all ways in which we assure that the people doing the work are integrally involved in the decisions about that work. Innovative care models are showing great promise in how care is delivered using the right people in the right places at the right time to provide care. Lessons learned during the pandemic should continue to inform how care is delivered going forward. Nursing schools tend to want high first-time pass rates for the NCLEX. To get them, they choose only the candidates with higher grade point averages (GPAs) and test scores, and that tends to be white females. Unfortunately, that does not represent the larger patient population. We must expand admission criteria and place less emphasis on GPA and first-time pass rates and more on the art and soft skills that nursing brings to the table. Education that incorporates compassion and empathy, not as phrases or buzzwords, makes patients feel safe while inspiring the caregiver. Storytelling during huddles, staff meetings, and town halls reaffirm the ability of caregivers to make a difference.

Nurse Engagement

Nurse engagement evolves from feeling safe and fulfilled in what you do, trusting your leaders and colleagues, recognition for doing a respectable job, and growing professionally. Nurses must practice in a safe environment, free from violence and degradation. They must be inspired to connect with their patients and colleagues in caring and compassionate ways—this is done by modeling behaviors in leadership and driving accountability not just for task accomplishment but for holistic care. Nurses must trust that their leaders fulfill the mission, vision, and values with integrity, transparency, honesty, and skill. They must feel a sense of belonging, an intrinsic motivator. In Maslow's Hierarchy of Needs, belonging is in the middle of the pyramid. Reaching the midpoint does not occur without safety, and that means feeling safe. In a 2020 study, people who feel like they belong said they were happier and had greater overall well-being and experienced a reduction in anxiety, depression, hopelessness, loneliness, social anxiety, and suicidal thoughts—all of which plague our nurses today.[3] Nurses must be recognized tangibly and intangibly for the work they do through fair and equitable compensation and recognition programs like the DAISY Award. We must offer time away to rest and recharge. Research has shown that people who don't get meal breaks are less likely to stay.[4] Extended work shifts (defined as 12.5 hours) are associated with increased errors, adverse events, and complications.[5] However, those increases drop when people are given breaks away from patient care throughout the shift. People need time away, especially in today's environment. Leaders need to make sure they get it. We need to applaud people for taking vacations, going to lunch off the unit, and taking a break away from patient care. Leaders should model that behavior—what's essential to the leader is important to staff. Finally, nurses must have the opportunity to grow and develop professionally through continuous learning, promotional opportunities, and skill acquisition.

Reflection

As I reflect on my career as a nurse, nurse leader, and educator, what would I tell my younger self in nursing school? Remember why you do what you do every day. The reward is not monetary, nor is it rec-ognition. Your work will be challenging, and you may want to leave. Remember your why—you make a difference every day in the lives of those for whom you care and with whom you work. You may not remember them, but they will remember you forever. You are caring for people at their most vulnerable time, and *you* will make the dif-ference. Don't lose hope.

Chapter 26

Nurses Hold the Keys for Fixing Broken Healthcare

Dina Readinger

Nurses hold the keys for fixing broken healthcare. Healthcare is plagued with bad decisions. The evidence shows that the workforce is overloaded and understaffed, and that we have poorly performing teams inside broken systems. The noncollaborating electronic medical record (EMR) leaves clinicians in the dark when patients need to choose physicians who live in other demographic locations; systems are failing from the start.

The Challenge

The result of this broken system has led to the inability of nurses to do their job the way they hoped. The nurse exodus will leave the healthcare system in shambles, and it all begins with solving the right problem at the right time. The nurse crisis is not new. Their cries for change have been clear for the last fifty years. Is anyone listening?

The Subconscious Mind

As humans, we continue to write our own programming by creating the narrative we want to believe is true, the self-talk that makes us comfortable with the uncomfortable, and we do not solve the right problem at the right time. Our beliefs about money, success, opportunity, and our future are sourced by the energy of our subconscious. The subconscious is thirty thousand times more powerful than the conscious mind; if we want to fix broken healthcare, we must focus on reprogramming broken thinking by solving the right problem at the right time.

The leader who keeps the broken thinking mind says, "Paying a nurse more creates retention." While pay might attract hires or locums to address healthcare demand, the decision to stay is often influenced by the work environment. Overwork and a dysfunctional team can dissuade individuals from remaining. Merely applying temporary fixes to problems is akin to exacerbating the issue. It leads to a lack of commitment to team and outcomes, creating a survival mentality. The contract nurse now breeds resentment among the loyal nurses within the system who are doing the same work for less money. Nurses feel trapped with no satisfactory solution except to "get out." Nurses want a place to work where they can do what they love to do, get paid their worth, and are given an opportunity to be effective. Nurses want flexibility, development, and a less stressful environment. They want to find a cure for healthcare's broken systems, but no one is listening to them.

Is There a Fix?

To fix broken healthcare, you must fix broken thinking. Employees within any system must feel that their ideas for change are valid while experimenting, confirming, and encouraging new ways to approach old and recent problems. The current healthcare situation is like a tumbleweed in the desert. It keeps rolling along as problems get bigger and as time goes on. The evidence is here. We know how to fix this issue by making sure we are solving the right problem at the right time. If we do not find the right problem and do not take the proper action now, costs for healthcare will continue to escalate, while the need for new nurses and clinicians continues to rise.

Broken thinking has created the perfect storm for healthcare today. Leaders must take an innovative approach and be held accountable for creating the new systems that nurses, clinicians, and healthcare workers need. Noncollaboration is costing systems billions of dollars through fragmented care, noncollaborating electronic medical records, reduced quality of care, limited access to specialty care, and waste due to inefficient processes and procedures.

The Key

Leaders must allow the nurses to step in and step up to be the change, acting on innovative ideas and making a way for healthcare to heal its brokenness. Peel off the Band-Aid and get to the root of fixing what is broken. It all begins with how we think. The biggest steps for overcoming the narrative of the subconscious mind are to bring small teams of people together, use the evidence in this book, and get to work. Solving the healthcare crisis begins with those who are doing the work, not the leaders. Great leaders allow great minds to change broken systems because they are addressing their own needs. Are you listening? It's time to think differently by design.

Reflection

My initial jump into healthcare was starting one of the first nuclear cardiology labs in the Midwest. I was introduced to the kindness and cruelty of healthcare. I worked for one of the brightest cardiologists around, but one who suffered from addiction and mental health issues. I feared losing a patient under his watch with zero control of the unanticipated outcome. It was grueling and heartbreaking. After ten years in the healthcare system, I decided that pharmaceutical sales for the next twenty-five years provided me a less stressful option, since most of my ten-hour days in the healthcare system were sixteen-plus hours with zero balance, little pay, and zero time for self-care.

Thirty-five years later, I found myself reflecting on what I could have done differently. Life was never meant to be lived alone. My wish to fix my own broken thinking led me to create Diagnostic Design Thinking to unleash the power of collective knowledge, transforming lives and careers, and making a difference. We can't fix broken thinking on our own because we are unaware of the things we can't see. Our own lack of confidence, fear of being wrong, fear of facing incivility, fear of speaking up may lead us to a spiral of hopelessness and unhappiness. We must arrest the subconscious so that we can unleash the right strategies at the right time. We must collaborate in safe spaces out of love for one another, not shaming or blaming but with a heartfelt need to help others and fix the brokenness deep within our souls, both as humans and within the bowels of healthcare.

Chapter 27

From Ideation to Reality

Sharon M. Weinstein

This book began with a nurse leader listening tour and asking the "Right Question!"

Early in 2023, Dina Readinger and I hosted a twice-weekly Nurse Leader Listening Tour . . . we asked lots of questions and received many answers. We invited our guests to engage with their peers and with us, as we addressed issues related to nurses, nursing, and the workforce. Our goal was to provide nurse leaders with an opportunity to be heard, express their opinions, share ideas, and tell their stories.

The Backstory

Through the culmination of hundreds of Diagnostic Thinking™ (DT) groups, which empower participants to jumpstart their thoughts, generate impact for their organizations, and foster ideation and innovation, we have observed that success hinges on *posing the right questions* and *addressing the right problems*. Principles gleaned from the

DT experience are applicable in all healthcare settings, and for clinicians at various stages of their careers. By creating an inclusive, psychologically safe work environment, we present an opportunity to unravel neural responses to events that might otherwise lead to feelings of being stuck, frustrated, and burned out. Nowhere is this more pertinent than in the healthcare sector.

The Discovery Process

Nurse leaders from academic and practice settings were eager to share their challenges, asking:

- How does the current environment contribute to, or detract from, the mission of improving the nation's health—one nurse at a time?
- What role does the healthcare environment play in recruitment and retention? Is it more than culture?
- What makes nurses stay in their jobs?
- How do we ensure psychological safety?
- Have you seen an increase in disruptive behavior since the pandemic?
- How are you addressing bullying and incivility?
- What's more important—disruptive behaviors, staffing, or burnout?
- Are nurses fighting for staff ratios—and can the fight be won?
- What gives you hope?
- What do you see for nursing's future?
- What would you tell a younger version of yourself?
- How do nurses own their values and practice?
- Why is nursing knowledge a public value?

- Did a setback redirect you in your career?
- How does innovation ensure a pipeline for our future?
- How can we support nursing teams to create a trusted space?
- How does nurses' health affect the quality and safety of care?
- How do we improve the state of health and well-being for healthcare staff?
- Who helped you along your journey to success?
- What work are you most proud of?
- How have you managed your own struggles with well-being?
- What are the drivers of long-term registered nurse (RN) retention?
- How are you as a leader addressing resilience and turnover?
- What do nurses need from us?
- How do you advocate for your team?

What Happens When You Ask the Right Question?

When we asked the right question at the right time, the well overflowed with comments, concerns, and ideas that resonated loudly and clearly. To take us to the next level, we needed to focus on Workplace, Well-Being, and Wisdom, and that is precisely what we have done!

Workforce: recruitment and retention require that we

- Grow our own nurses

- Remain flexible
- Listen with intention
- Offer support
- Reduce fractionation
- Dissolve cognitive dissonance

Well-Being: a healthy work environment

- Promotes nurse health
- Ensures psychological and physical safety
- Supports a mindset that brings smiles each day
- Offers self-care and well-being for all nurses
- Moves from a crisis-care system to a wellness and prevention system

Wisdom: mandates that we

- Give nurses a voice
- Lead with a bottom-up, side-to-side, and top-down approach
- Identify needs and solve one problem at a time
- Find resources that can break down barriers
- Ensure that nurses know that they matter
- Set new nurses up for success
- Employ evidence-based interventions to heal healthcare

Beyond the clinical and academic spaces, providers face challenges in creating a clear career path, being the new member of a team, feeling valued, and much more. As we transition from a lingering pandemic to what lies ahead, what will your thought process be? Are you ready to think differently, ask the right questions, and solve the right problems?

Reflection

I ask myself, "If I knew then what I know now, would my journey have been the same?" My own four-decade nursing career began with a diploma program and, following marriage and three (now-adult) children who have produced families of their own, my return to school for baccalaureate and master's programs, culminating in the Executive Program at the Kellogg School. Along this diverse path, I had the privilege of serving as the president of my professional nursing society and chair of the certification board. I also led delegations of infusion professionals across the globe, testified for both plaintiffs and defendants in legal cases involving my specialty practice area, and contributed to establishing the healthcare infrastructure in the newly developed countries of the former Soviet Union.

I never thought much about asking the right question, or solving for x. Confronted with a challenge, whether identified by others or arising from my own observations, I instinctively sought and implemented effective solutions. My approach is consistently aimed at resolving issues, expanding services, ensuring quality, and guaranteeing great outcomes.

However, absent the benefit of a DT group, I made mistakes along the way and allowed limiting beliefs to hold me back. Imagine what I could have done, and imagine how I could have shortened my trajectory, had I known then what I know now. I am grateful to Dina Readinger for introducing me to the concept of untangling from old assumptions to embrace a new way of thinking . . . one that gets to the core of posing the right question to solve the right problem at the right time!

Postscript

We feel certain *Healing Healthcare* is destined to become a part of our toolbox that will guide our respective futures. Another special thank you to Bernadette M. Melnyk and Katie Boston-Leary for their contributions to a book of which we are so proud. Again, we want to acknowledge our contributing authors for sharing their time, talent, and evidence with us through the Nurse Leader Listening Tour, personal interviews, and now—our collective book. These brilliant educators, clinicians, and leaders from the healthcare space have given you, the reader, a chance to reflect on what has worked, will work, and perhaps what needs to happen next in our quest toward *Healing Healthcare*. We highlight their nuggets here!

Workforce

- Encourage early exposure to our profession, get the word out, and create school advocacy programs for healthcare professionals.
- Diversity and inclusion should mirror the population.
- Streamline education, making it accessible, affordable, and less punitive.
- Focus on retention vs. dropping out.
- Create nurse advocacy programs.
- Create self-care programs.
- Fight for flexible work hours.
- Develop opportunities for everyone.
- Foster and reward teamwork and collaboration.
- Be better listeners.
- Ask others to think differently, track results, and be open to innovative ideas.
- Spend time with those on the front lines—ask, listen, and learn.
- Actively talk about mental health, making it easy to bring up and address the needs of nurses.
- Actively protect the safety of nurses.
- Proactively offer programs to address depression, PTSD, and stress.
- Address . . . don't assume.
- Practice radical transparency.
- Show up.
- Find any excuse to celebrate.
- Double down on culture.

Well-Being

- Reduce the unrelenting tasks not relevant to nursing to provide top-notch patient care.
- Integrate health and wellness programs giving nurses a safety net and a reason to stay.
- Create policies for work-life balance.
- Prioritize well-being and ask nurses what they need to feel well cared for.
- Create a nurse suicide prevention program.
- Empower nurses to step in when crisis occurs and support the frontline staff.
- Be intentional about supporting the physical and emotional needs of nurses.
- Restore joy in the workplace.
- Create a call to action for compassionate care for patients, self, and one another.
- Create burnout and retention programs; address the onset of burnout.

Wisdom

- Develop innovative critical-thinking programs that evaluate, discern, challenge, and master new and innovative ways to manage self and others.
- Harvest broad knowledge: find mentors who love to develop others and pay it forward.
- Stay ahead of technical expertise with holistic patient care and ethical decision-making.

- Create platforms that share interdisciplinary knowledge and ways that other nurses can share their personal wisdom to create the change they need today.
- Nurses must advocate for themselves and each other and collaboratively find the right solution to the right problem.

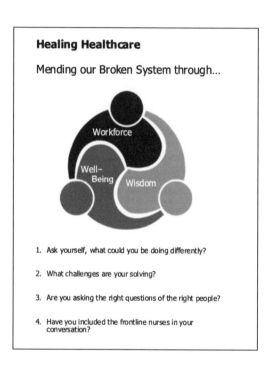

Healing Healthcare

Mending our Broken System through...

Workforce

Well-Being

Wisdom

1. Ask yourself, what could you be doing differently?

2. What challenges are your solving?

3. Are you asking the right questions of the right people?

4. Have you included the frontline nurses in your conversation?

Take these golden nuggets and create initiatives that work within your own organization or health system. We challenge you to be the rainmakers . . . the keys to our future and the drivers of change using evidence-based strategies to mend our broken system through Workforce, Well-Being, and Wisdom! It's up to you to take ownership of the healthcare system, to build a workforce that works and workplaces that support nurses' well-being. It's up to you to stop grasping for quick fixes and to apply the evidence-based strategies that will heal healthcare. It's up to you to covet the words of wisdom shared by our contributors. Let us be your guides as you press reset and begin the journey of a lifetime!

We are so pleased to have the opportunity to expand our reach beyond the business, pharmaceutical, and life sciences fields to collaborate with educational institutions like Purdue Global University and others to identify and solve the right problems at the right time. We'd like to introduce the DDTG process to you and your team. To get started, visit thinkdifferentlybydesign.com and schedule a workshop for your organization. This is the first step on the journey to Thinking Differently, and it begins and ends with you.

Endnotes

Dedication

1   Stembridge, E. (2021). "Standing Ovation" mural unveiled
    in honor of National Nurses Week. *VUMC Voice*. https://
    voice.vumc.org/standing-ovation-mural-unveiled-in-honor-of-
    national-nurses-week

Foreword – Katie Boston-Leary

1   Healthcare Plus Solutions Group. (2023). National models
    of care insight study results, in collaboration with ANA and
    AONL. https://healthcareplussg.com/models-of-care-insight-
    study

Introduction

1   Porter, M. E., & Lee, T. H. (2013). The strategy that will
    fix health care. *Harvard Business Review*. https://hbr.
    org/2013/10/the-strategy-that-will-fix-health-care

2   Elsevier Health. (2023). Clinician of the future 2023: Education edition. Elsevier.

3   Lee, K. A., & Friese, C. R. (2021). Deaths by suicide among nurses: A rapid response call. *Journal of Psychosocial Nursing and Mental Health Services, 59*(8), 3–4. https://doi. org/10.3928/02793695-20210625-01

Chapter 2

1   American Association of Nurse Anesthetists. (2023). History of nurse anesthesia practice. AANA. https://www.aana.com/about-us/history

2   American Association of Nurse Practitioners. (2023). NP fact sheet. AANP. https://www.aanp.org/about/all-about-nps/np-fact-sheet

3   American College of Nurse-Midwives. (2023). History of midwifery and ACNM. ACNM. https://www.midwife.org/our-history

4   Fulton, J. S., Lyon, B. L., & Goudreau, K. A. (Eds.). (2010). *Foundations of clinical nurse specialist practice.* Springer Publishing Company.

5   Phillips, S. J. (2022). 34th annual APRN legislative update: Trends in APRN practice authority during the COVID-19 global pandemic. *Nurse Practitioner, 47*(1), 21–47.

6   Feyereisen, S., & Puro, N. (2020). Seventeen states enacted executive orders expanding advanced practice nurses' scopes of practice during the first 21 days of the COVID-19 pandemic. *Rural and Remote Health, 20*(4), 1–4.

7   Greenhalgh, T., Wherton, J., Shaw, S., & Morrison, C. (2020). Video consultations for COVID-19. *BMJ, 368.*

8   Buerhaus, P. I., Skinner, L. E., Auerbach, D. I., & Staiger, D. O. (2015). Four challenges facing the nursing workforce in the United States. *Journal of Nursing Regulation, 6*(2), 40–46.

9   Phillips, S. J. (2021). 33rd annual APRN legislative update: Unprecedented changes to APRN practice authority in unprecedented times. *Nurse Practitioner, 46*(1), 27–55.

10 Delaney, L. J. (2018). Patient-centered care as an approach to improving healthcare in Australia. *Collegian, 25*(1), 119–123.

11 Woo, B. F., Poon, S. N., Tam, W. W., & Zhou, W. (2022). The impact of COVID19 on advanced practice nursing education and practice: A qualitative study. *International Nursing Review, 69*(3), 330–339.

12 Kleinpell, R. M. (Ed.). (2021). *Outcome assessment in advanced practice nursing* (5th ed.). Springer Publishing Company.

13 Galanis, P., Vraka, I., Fragkou, D., Bilali, A., & Kaitelidou, D. (2021). Nurses' burnout and associated risk factors during the COVID-19 pandemic: A systematic review and meta-analysis. *Journal of Advanced Nursing, 77*(8), 3286–3302.

Chapter 3

1   Cox, S. (2018). The power of gratitude. *Nursing Management, 49*(4), 56.

Chapter 4

1   Akparewa, N. E. (2021). *The clinician's guide to microaggressions & unconscious bias: Racial justice in healthcare.*

2   Flath, L. A., Schwartz, D. E., & VanGelder, A. (2023). Corporate DEI policies face scrutiny following SCOTUS affirmative action decision. https://www.skadden.com/insights/publications/2023/09/quarterly-insights/corporate-dei-polices-face-scrutiny

Chapter 5

1   Munro, C. L., & Hope, A. A. (2020). Healthy work environ-
    ment: Resolutions for 2020. *American Journal of Critical
    Care, 29*(1), 4–6.

2   Mohr, D. C., Burgess, J. F., Jr., & Young, G. J. (2008). The
    influence of teamwork culture on physician and nurse resigna-
    tion rates in hospitals. *Health Services Management Research,
    21*(1), 23–31.

3   Carlisle, B., Perera, A., Stutzman, S., Brown-Cleere, S., Par-
    waiz, A., & Olson, D. (2020). Efficacy of using available data
    to examine nurse staffing ratios and quality of care metrics.
    Journal of Neuroscience Nursing, 52(2), 78–83. doi:10.1097/
    JNN.0000000000000499

4   Bowie, B., & Baker, K. (2019). Centralized vs. decentralized
    staffing: Two case studies. *American Nurse 14*(6), 41–47.

5   Newby, J. C., Mabry, M. C., Carlisle, B. A., Olson, D. M., &
    Lane, B. E. (2020). Reflections on nursing ingenuity during
    the COVID-19 pandemic. *Journal of Neuroscience Nursing,
    52*(5), E13–E16. doi:10.1097/jnn.0000000000000525

6   Boston-Fleischhauer, C. (2020). Leading through crisis: Sup-
    porting your workforce and shoring up staff resiliency during
    COVID-19 [PowerPoint slides].

Chapter 6

1   Aiken, L. H., Clarke, S. P., & Sloane, D. M. (2002). Hospital
    staffing, organization, and quality of care: Cross-national find-
    ings. *International Journal for Quality in Health Care, 14*(1),
    5–13. http://www.jstor.org/stable/45125740

Chapter 7

1   Clifton, J. (2022). Gallup global emotions 2022. Gallup. https://img.lalr.co/cms/2022/06/29185719/2022-Gallup-Global-Emotions-Report-2022_compressed.pdf

2   Clifton, J., & Harter, J. (2023). *Culture shock: An unstoppable force is changing how we work and live.* Gallup Press.

3   Tye, J. (2020) Living your values. *Nurse Leader, 18(1),* 67.

4   Tye, J. (2020). Living your values. *Nurse Leader, 18(1),* 67–72.

5   Trusted Health. (2021). Frontline nurse mental health and well-being survey. Trusted Health.

6   Dixon, N. (2016). *On the psychology of military incompetence.* Basic Books.

7   Stack, J. (2003). *A stake in the outcome: Building a culture of ownership for the long-term success of your business.* Currency.

8   Tye, J. (2023). *How the DAISY foundation has influenced the global healthcare landscape* (2nd ed.). Values Coach, Inc.

9   Pfeffer, J. (2018). *Dying for a paycheck: How modern management harms employee health and company performance—and what we can do about it.* HarperCollins.

Chapter 8

1   Melnyk, B. M., & Raderstorf, T. C. (Eds.). (2021). *Evidence-based leadership, innovation and entrepreneurship in nursing and healthcare: A practical guide for success.* Springer Publishing Company.

2   Raderstorf, T. C., Melnyk, B. M., Ackerman, M., & Bibyk, S. (2020). An outcomes evaluation of makerspace programming on interprofessional learning, job satisfaction and intent to stay among clinicians. *JONA, 50(2):*109–114.

3   Ackerman, M. H., Giuliano, K. K., & Malloch, K. (2020). The novation dynamic: Clarifying the work of change, disruption, and innovation. *Nurse Leader, 18*(3), 232–236.

4   Yen, P. Y., Kellye, M., Lopetegui, M., Saha, A., Loversidge, J., Chipps, E. M., Gallagher-Ford, L., & Buck, J. (2018). Nurses' time allocation and multitasking of nursing activities: A time motion study. *AMIA Annual Symposium Proceedings. AMIA Symposium 2018*, 1137–1146.

5   Overhage, J. M., & McCallie, D. (2020). Physician time spent using the electronic health record during outpatient encounters. *Annals of Internal Medicine, 172*(3), 169–174.

6   Williams, M., & Filby, M. (2022, July 7). OhioHealth to eliminate 637 jobs in its biggest layoff ever. *Columbus Dispatch*. https://www.dispatch.com/story/business/2022/07/07/ohio-health-announces-biggest-layoff-company-history/7829847001

7   Leonard, A. (2023). Dr. Google meets its match in diagnosing symptoms: Dr. Chatbot. *Health Florida News*. https://wusf-news.wusf.usf.edu/health-news-florida/2023-09-17/dr-google-meets-its-match-in-diagnosing-symptoms-dr-chatbot

8   Rometty, G. (2021). Growth and comfort do not coexist. Laidlaw Scholars Network.

9   Leary, M. (2021). Design thinking for nurses: A new course teaches students one of the most effective systems for innovation. https://www.nursing.upenn.edu/details/news.php?id=1369

10   Readinger, D., & Weinstein, S. M. (2022). *Think Differently by Design*: Rockville, SMW Group Publishing.

Chapter 9

1   NDNQI. (2023). National database for nursing quality indicators. Press Ganey.

2 Advisory Board. (2023). Recommendations for stabilizing the RN workforce. *Advisory Board.*

3 Chicca, J., & Shellenbarger, T. (2018). Connecting with generation Z: Approaches in nursing education. *Teaching and Learning in Nursing, 13*(3), 180–184. doi:https://doi.org/10.1016/j.teln.2018.03.008

4 Hampton, D., & Welsh, D. (2019). Work values of generation Z nurses. *Journal of Nursing Administration, 49*(10), 480–486. doi:10.1097/NNA.0000000000000791

5 Sherman, R. O. (2021). Keeping an eye on generation Z nurses. *Nurse Leader, 19*(1), 6–7. https://doi.org/10.1016/j.mnl.2020.11.001

6 Sherman, R. O. (2021). Keeping an eye on generation Z nurses. *Nurse Leader, 19(I),* 6.

Chapter 10

1 Advisory Board. (2022). RN market outlook. *Advisory Board.*

2 McKinsey & Company. (2023). Nursing in 2023: How hospitals are confronting shortages. McKinsey & Company. https://www.mckinsey.com/~/media/mckinsey/industries/healthcare%20systems%20and%20services/our%20insights/nursing%20in%202023/nursing-in-2023-how-hospitals-are-confronting-shortages_final.pdf

3 Boston-Fleischhauer, C., and Whitemarsh, K. (2022). Hard truths on the current and future state of the nursing workforce. *Advisory Board.*

4 Maslach, C., & Leiter, M. P. (2016). Burnout. In Fink, F. (Ed.), *Stress: Concepts, cognition, emotion, and behavior* (pp. 351–357). Academic Press.

5   Kelly, L. A., Weston, M. J., & Gee, P. M. (2021). A nurse leader's guide to reducing burnout: Strategies to improve well-being. *Nurse Leader, 19*(5), 467–473.

6   Aiken, L. H., Lasater, K. B., Sloane, D. M., Pogue, C. A., Fitzpatrick Rosenbaum, K. E., Muir, K. J., & McHugh, M. D. (2023). Physician and nurse wellbeing and preferred interventions to address burnout in hospital practice. *JAMA Health Forum, 4*(7), e231809. doi:10.1001/jamahealthforum.2023.1809

7   Colosi, B. (2023). 2023 NSI national health care retention and RN staffing report. NSI Nursing Solutions, Inc. https://www.nsinursingsolutions.com/Documents/Library/NSI_National_Health_Care_Retention_Report.pdf

8   West, C. P., Dyrbye, L. N., Erwin, P. J., & Shanafelt, T. D. (2016). Interventions to prevent and reduce physician burnout: A systematic review and meta-analysis. *Lancet, 388*(10057), 2272–2281.

9   Panagioti, M., Panagopoulou, E., Bower, P., et al. (2017). Controlled interventions to reduce burnout in physicians: A systematic review and meta-analysis. *JAMA Internal Medicine, 177*(2), 195–205.

10   Aiken, L. H., Lasater, K. B., Sloane, D. M., Pogue, C. A., Fitzpatrick-Rosenbaum, E. E., Muir, K. J., & McHugh, M. D. (2023). Physician and nurse well-being and preferred interventions to address burnout in hospital practice. *JAMA Health Forum, 47*(7), E231809. DOI:10.1001/JAMAHEALTHFORUM.2023.1809

11   Ulrich, B., Cassidy, L., Barden, C., Varn-Davis, N., & Delgado, S. A. (2022). National nurse work environments – October 2021: A status report. *Critical Care Nurse, 42*(5), 58–70. https://doi.org/10.4037/ccn2022798

12 American Nurses Foundation. (2022). Mental health and wellness survey. https://www.nursingworld.org/practice-policy/work-environment/health-safety/disaster-preparedness/coronavirus/what-you-need-to-know/pulse-on-the-nations-nurses-covid-19-survey-series-mental=health-and-wellness-survey-3-september-2021. Accessed July 6, 2023

13 American Association of Critical-Care Nurses. (2016). AACN standards for establishing and sustaining healthy work environments. AACN. https://www.aacn.org/~/media/aacn-website/nursing-excellence/standards/hwestandards.pdf

14 Buerhaus, P., Fraher, E., Frogner, B., Buntin, M., O'Reilly-Jacob, M., and Clarke, S. (2023). Toward a stronger post-pandemic nursing workforce. *N Engl J Med, 389(3)*, 200–203.

15 Rocchio, B. J., Seys, J. D., Willliams, D. L., Vancil, B. J., & McNett, M. M. (2022). The post-pandemic nursing workforce: Increasing fill rates and reducing workload through a generational design of workforce layers. *Nurs Adm Q, 47(1)*, 4–12.

16 Advisory Board. (2023). Recommendations for stabilizing the RN workforce. *Advisory Board.*

17 Berlin, G., Bilazarian, A., Chang, J., & Hammer, S. (2023). Reimagining the nursing workload: Finding time to close the workforce gap. McKinsey & Company. https://www.mckinsey.com/industries/healthcare/our-insights/reimagining-the-nursing-workload-finding-time-to-close-the-workforce-gap

18 Roccio, B. J., Sweys, J. D., Williams, D. L., Vancil, B. J., & McNett, M. M. (2022). The post-pandemic nursing workforce: Increasing fill rates and reducing workload through a generational design of workforce layers. *Nurs Adm Q, 47(1)*, 4–12.

Chapter 11

1   Keng, S. L., Stanton, M. V., Haskins, L. B., et al. (2022). CO-
    VID-19 stressors, and health behaviors: A multilevel longitu-
    dinal study across 86 countries. *Prev Med Rep, 27*, 101764.
    doi:10.1016/j.pmedr.2022.101764

2   Schmidt, R. A., Genois, R., Jin, J., Vigo, D., Rehm, J., &
    Rush, B. (2021). The early impact of COVID-19 on the inci-
    dence, prevalence, and severity of alcohol use and other drugs:
    A systematic review. *Drug Alcohol Depend, 228*, 109065.
    doi:10.1016/j.drugalcdep.2021.109065

3   Centers for Disease Control and Prevention. (2023). How you
    can prevent chronic disease. CDC. https://www.cdc.gov/chron-
    icdisease/about/prevent/index.htm

4   Office of the Surgeon General. (2022). Addressing health
    worker burnout: The US surgeon general's advisory on build-
    ing a thriving health workforce. US Department of Health and
    Human Services. https://www.hhs.gov/surgeongeneral/priori-
    ties/health-worker-burnout/index.html

5   Han, S., Shanafelt, T. D., Sinsky, C. A., et al. (2019). Estimat-
    ing the attributable cost of physician burnout in the United
    States. *Ann Intern Med, 170*(11), 784–790. doi:10.7326/M18-
    1422

6   National Academy of Medicine. Action collaborative on clini-
    cian well-being and resilience. National Academy of Medicine.
    https://nam.edu/initiatives/clinician-resilience-and-well-being

7   Amaya, M., Battista, L., & Melnyk, B. (2018). The Ohio State
    University's strategic approach to improving total population
    health. *American Journal of Health Promotion, 32*(8), 1823–
    1826. doi:10.1177/0890117118804149e

8   The Ohio State University Health and Wellness. (2022). Well-
     ness strategic plan. https://wellness.osu.edu/chief-wellness-
     officer/wellness-strategic-plan

9   Fox, W. A. (2020). The emergence of the chief wellness officer
     in US higher education (Dissertation). University of Pittsburgh.
     https://d-scholarship.pitt.edu/39947/1/Fox_ETD_2020_dschol.
     pdf

10   Melnyk, B. M. Improving population health and well-being
     in academic institutions and healthcare systems with the chief
     wellness officer: A vital yet untapped nursing leadership role.
     Nursing Outlook (in press).

11   Melnyk, B. M., Hsieh, A. P., Tan, A., et al. (2022). Associa-
     tions among nurses' mental/physical health, lifestyle behaviors,
     shift length, and workplace wellness support during CO-
     VID-19: Important implications for health care systems. *Nurs
     Adm Q*, 46(1), 5–18. doi:10.1097/NAQ.0000000000000499

12   Melnyk, B. M., Hsieh, A. P., Tan, A., et al. (2023). The state
     of health, burnout, healthy behaviors, workplace wellness sup-
     port, and concerns of medication errors in pharmacists during
     the COVID-19 pandemic. *J Occup Environ Med*, 65(8),
     699–705. doi:10.1097/JOM.0000000000002889

13   Cappelucci, K., Zindel, M., Knight, H. C., Busis, N., &
     Alexander, C. (2019). Clinician well-being at Ohio State
     University: A case study. *NAM Perspectives*. https://doi.
     org/10.31478/201908b https://wellness.osu.edu/buckeye-well-
     ness/buckeye-wellness-innovators

14   Melnyk, B. M., Strait, L. A., Beckett, C., Hsieh, A. P., Mess-
     inger, J., & Masciola, R. (2023). The state of mental health,
     burnout, mattering and perceived wellness culture in doctor-
     ally prepared nursing faculty with implications for action

[published correction appears in *Worldviews Evid Based Nurs,* 20(4), 415]. *Worldviews Evid Based Nurs,* 20(2), 142–152. doi:10.1111/wvn.12632

15 Mitchell, L., Amaya, M., Battista, L., Melnyk, B., Andridge, R., & Kaye, G. (2021). Manager support for wellness champions: A case study for consideration and practice implications. *Workplace Health Saf,* 69(3), 100–108. doi:10.1177/2165079920952759

16 Amaya, M. E., Melnyk, B. M., Buffington, B., & Battista, L. (2017). Workplace wellness champions: Lessons learned and implications for future programming. *BHAC Journal, 1*(1), 59–67.

17 Amaya, M., Battista, L., & Melnyk, B. (2018). The Ohio State University's strategic approach to improving total population health. *Am J Health Promot, 32*(8), 1823–1826. doi:10.1177/0890117118804149e

Chapter 12

1   Advisory Board. (2023). Charted: The most trusted professions in America according to Gallup. *Advisory Board.* https://www.advisory.com/daily-briefing/2023/01/18/trusted-professionals

2   ANA Enterprise. (2023). Healthy nurse, healthy nation. https://www.healthynursehealthynation.org

3   Patrician, P., Bakerjian, D., Billings, R., Chenot, T. Hooper, V., Johnson, C., & Sables-Baus, S. (2022). Nurse well-being: A concept analysis. *Nursing Outlook, 70*(4), 639–650.

4   Patrician, P., Bakerjian, D., Billings, R. C., Hopper, V., Johnson, C., & Sables-Baus, S. (2022). Nurse well-being: A concept analysis *Nursing Outlook, 70(4), 640.*

5   Johnson, S., & Dickerson, P. (2022). *Journey to Equity*. ANA Nursing Knowledge Center.

6   Roberts, P. (2018). Three good things build resilience and improve well-being. *American Nurse Today, 13*(12), 26–29.

7   Johnson, S., and Dickerson, P. (2022). *Journey to Equity*. ANA Nursing Knowledge Center.

8   Roberts, P. (2018) Three good things build resilience and improve well-being. *American Nurse Today, 13*(12), 26–29.

9   Roberts, P. (2018) Three good things build resilience and improve well-being. *American Nurse Today, 13*(12), 27.

10 Armenta, C. N., Fritz, M. M., Lyubomirsky, S. (2017). Functions of positive emotions: Gratitude as a motivator of self-improvement and positive change. *Emotion Review, 9*(3), 183–90.

Chapter 13

1   Cubillos, L., & Lawhorn, C. on behalf of the Center for Global Mental Health Research and Global Mental Health Team. (2023). Going global: Advancing mental health research around the world. nih.gov

2   Centers for Disease Control and Prevention. https://www.cdc.gov/hrqol/wellbeing.htm; https://www.cdc.gov/workplacehealthpromotion/initiatives/resource-center/case-studies/engage-employees-health-wellness.html

Chapter 14

1   Naegle, M. A., Kelly, L. A., Embree, J. L. Valentine, N., Sharp, D., Grinspun, D., Hines-Martin, V. P., Crawford, C. L., & Rosa, W. E. (2023). American Academy of Nursing consensus recommendations to advance system level change for nurse well-being. *Nursing Outlook, 71*(2), 101917.

2   American Nurses Association. (2022). Partners for nurse
    staffing think tank nurse staffing think tank: Priority top-
    ics and recommendations. ANA. https://www.nursingworld.
    org/~49940b/globalassets/practiceandpolicy/nurse-staffing/
    nurse-staffing-think-tank-recommendation.pdf

Chapter 15

1   Lluch, C., Galiana, L., Doménech, P., & Sansó, N. (2022).
    The impact of the COVID-19 pandemic on burnout, compas-
    sion fatigue, and compassion satisfaction in healthcare per-
    sonnel: A systematic review of the literature published during
    the first year of the pandemic. *Healthcare (Basel), 10*(2), 364.
    https://doi.org/10.3390/healthcare10020364

2   Ulrich, B., Cassidy, L., Barden, C., Varn-Davis, N., & Delga-
    do, S. A. (2022). National nurse work environments – Octo-
    ber 2021: A status report. *Critical Care Nurse, 42*(5), 58–70.
    https://doi.org/10.4037/ccn2022798

3   Martin, B., Kaminski-Ozturk, N., O'Hara, C., & Smiley, R.
    (2023). Examining the impact of the COVID-19 pandemic
    on burnout and stress among US nurses. *Journal of Nurs-
    ing Regulation, 14*(1), 4–12. https://doi.org/10.1016/S2155-
    8256(23)00063-7

4   Mohammed, S., Peter, E., Killackey, T., & Maciver, J. (2021).
    The "nurse as hero" discourse in the COVID-19 pandemic:
    A poststructural discourse analysis. *International journal
    of nursing studies, 117*, 103887. https://doi.org/10.1016/j.
    ijnurstu.2021.103887

5   American Nurses Association. (2019). ANA issue brief on
    reporting incidents of workplace violence. ANA. https://www.
    nursingworld.org/~495349/globalassets/docs/ana/ethics/enda-
    buse-issue-brief-final.pdf

6   Walsh, E., Greider, H., & Ridling, D. (2022). Tea for the soul:
    An intervention to support nurse resilience. *Nursing Manage-
    ment, 53*(12), 37–45.

7   Leamy, M., Reynolds, E., Robert, G., Taylor, C., & Maben,
    J. (2019). The origins and implementation of an interven-
    tion to support healthcare staff to deliver compassionate care:
    Exploring fidelity and adaptation in the transfer of Schwartz
    Center Rounds® from the United States to the United King-
    dom. *BMC Health Services Research, 19*(1), 457. https://doi.
    org/10.1186/s12913-019-4311-y

8   Von Visger, T. T., Thrane, S. E., Klatt, M. D., Chang, Y. P., &
    Happ, M. (2021). Deep relaxation experience with comple-
    mentary urban Zen integrative therapy: Qualitative thematic
    analysis. *Western Journal of Nursing Research, 43*(8), 723–
    731. https://doi.org/10.1177/0193945920973941

9   Melnyk, B. M., Tan, A., Hsieh, A. P., Gawlik, K., Arslanian-
    Engoren, C., Braun, L. T., Dunbar, S., Dunbar-Jacob, J.,
    Lewis, L. M., Millan, A., Orsolini, L., Robbins, L. B., Russell,
    C. L., Tucker, S., & Wilbur, J. (2021). Critical care nurses'
    physical and mental health, worksite wellness support, and
    medical errors. *American Journal of Critical Care, 30*(3),
    176–184. https://doi.org/10.4037/ajcc2021301

10 American Association of Critical-Care Nurses. (2023). AACN
    Healthy Work Environment resources. AACN. https://www.
    aacn.org/nursing-excellence/healthy-work-environments

Chapter 16

1   Hill, L., Artiga, S., & Ndugga, N. (2023). Covid-19 cases,
    deaths, and vaccinations by race/ethnicity as of winter 2022.
    KFF.

2   American Nurses Foundation. (2022). Pulse on the Nation's Nurses survey series: 2022 workplace survey. ANF. https://www.nursingworld.org/~4a209f/globalassets/covid19/anf-2022-workforce-written-report-final.pdf

3   Bianchi, R., Schonfeld, I. S., & Laurent, E. (2019). Burnout: Moving beyond the status quo. *International Journal of Stress Management, 26*(1), 36–45. https://doi.org/10.1037/str0000088

4   Flynn, J. (2023). 15+ nursing burnout statistics [2023]: The shocking truth about nursing. Zippia. https://www.zippia.com/advice/nursing-burnout-statistics

5   World Health Organization. (2019). Burn-out an "occupational phenomenon": International classification of diseases. https://www.who.int/news/item/28-05-2019-burn-out-an-occupational-phenomenon-international-classification-of-diseases

6   Jangir, V. (2018). Steve Jobs's last words. *Medium.* https://medium.com/@vikasjangir/steve-jobs-last-words-d79012fad236

Chapter 18

1   American Association of Critical-Care Nurses. (2023). AACN healthy work environment resources. AACN. https://www.aacn.org/nursing-excellence/healthy-work-environments

2   Clifton, J. (2022). Gallup global emotions 2022. Gallup. https://img.lalr.co/cms/2022/06/29185719/2022-Gallup-Global-Emotions-Report-2022_compressed.pdf

3   Trzeciak, S. & Mazzarelli, A. (2019). Compassionomics: The revolutionary scientific evidence that caring makes a difference. The Studer Group.

Chapter 19

1   Patel, H. Y., & West, D. J. (2021). Hospital at home: An
    evolving model for comprehensive healthcare. *Global Journal
    on Quality and Safety in Healthcare, 4*(4), 1141–1146. https://
    doi.org/10.36401/JQSH-21-4

2   Schuchman, M., Fain, M., & Cornwell, T. (2018). The resur-
    gence of home-based primary care models in the United States.
    Geriatrics (Basel), 3(3), 41. doi:10.3390/geriatrics3030041

3   Singh, J., Albertson, A., & Sillerud, B. (2022). Telemedicine
    during COVID-19 crisis and in post- pandemic/post-vaccine
    world: Historical overview, current utilization, and innova-
    tive practices to increase utilization. *Healthcare (Basel), 10*(6),
    1041. https://doi.org/10.3390/healthcare10061041

4   Colacino, C. (2017). Medicine in a changing world:
    2016–2017 Alvin F. Poussaint, MD visiting lecturer
    Martin-J. Sepúlveda shares insights. Harvard Medical
    School. https://hms.harvard.edu/news/medicine-changing-
    world#:~:text=In%20science%2C%20the%20term%20
    %E2%80%9Chalf,will%20be%20only%2073%20days

5   Nesbitt, T. S. (2012). The evolution of telehealth: Where have
    we been and where are we going? In *The role of telehealth in
    an evolving health care environment: Workshop summary.*
    Board on Healthcare Services, Institute of Medicine, Washing-
    ton (DC): National Academies Press. https://www.ncbi.nlm.
    nih.gov/books/NBK207141

6   Shaver, J. (2022). The state of telehealth before and after
    the COVIC-19 pandemic. *Primary Care, 49*(4), 517–530.
    doi:10.1016/j.pop.2022.04.002

7   World Health Organization. (2023). *Emerging technologies
    and scientific innovations: A global public health perspective.*
    WHO.

Chapter 20

1 McGuinness, T. (2021). Suicide: A dark cloud over nursing. American Association of Critical-Care Nurses. https://www. aacn.org/blog/suicide-a-dark-cloud-over-nursing

2 Tucker, S., Carpenter, H., & Mujic, A. (2023). Preventing nurse suicide: Nursing school and beyond. *American Nurse Journal, 18*(9), 78–80. https://www.myamericannurse.com/ preventing-nurse-suicide-nursing-school-and-beyond

3 Al-Qadi, M. M. (2021). Workplace violence in nursing: A concept analysis. *Journal of Occupational Health, 63*(1). https:// doi.org/10.1002/1348-9585.12226

Chapter 21

1 American Nurses Association. (2023). Nurses in the workforce. ANA. https://www.nursingworld.org/practice-pollicy/ workforce/

2 American Nurses Association. (2023). Nurses in the workforce. ANA. https://www.nursingworld.org/practice-policy/ workforce

3 Centers for Medicare and Medicaid Services. (2023). NHE fact sheet. CMS. https://www.cms.gov/data-research/statistics-trends-and-reports/national-health-expenditure-data/nhe-fact-sheet

4 American Association of Critical-Care Nurses. (2023). Nursing shortage fact sheet. AACN. https://www.aacnnursing.org/ news-information/fact-sheets/nursing-shortage

5 Brenan, M. (2023). Nurses retain top ethics rating in US, but below 2020 high. Gallup. https://news.gallup.com/ poll/467804/nurses-retain-top-ethics-rating-below-2020-high. aspx

6   Bureau of Labor Statistics, US Department of Labor. (2023). Registered nurses. In *Occupational outlook handbook*. https://www.bls.gov/ooh/healthcare/registered-nurses. htm#tab-6

Chapter 22

1   Yen, P. Y., Kellye, M., Lopetegui, M., Saha, A., Loversidge, J., Chipps, E. M., Gallagher-Ford, L., & Buck, J. Nurses' time allocation and multitasking of nursing activities: A time motion study. *AMIA Annu Symp Proc, 2018*, 1137–1146. PMID:30815156; PMCID:PMC6371290

2   Bartholomew, K., (2014). *Ending nurse to nurse hostility*. HCPro.

3   Pearson, C., & Porath, C. (2009). *The costs of bad behavior: How incivility is damaging your business and what to do about it* (2nd ed.). Portfolio.

4   Goleman, D. (2007). *Emotional intelligence* (10th ed.). Bantam Books.

5   Bartholomew, K. (2021). By design: Aligning values to improve outcomes in a public utility model. *Journal of Public Health International, 4*(3), 15–21.

6   Berwick, D. M. (2023). Salve lucrum: The existential threat of greed in US healthcare. *JAMA, 329*(8), 629–630. doi:10.1001/jama.2023.0846

7   Bartholomew, K. (2023). A care plan for nursing. *International Journal for Human Caring, 27*(3), 179–186. doi:10.20467/IJHC-2022-0002

Chapter 24

1   Evans, K. (2018). *Transforming healthcare: Healing you, me, and our broken disease-care system*. Butler Books.

2   Laires, P. A., Dias, S., Gama, A., Moniz, M., Pedro, A. R., Soares, P., Aguiar, P., & Nunes, C. (2021). The association between chronic disease and serious COVID-19 outcomes and its influence on risk perception: Survey study and database analysis. *JMIR Public Health Surveill, 7*(1), e22794. doi:10.2196/22794 PMID:33433397; PMCID:PMC7806339

3   Washington State Department of Health. (2023). COVID-19 hospitalizations and deaths by vaccination status in Washington State. https://doh.wa.gov/sites/default/files/2022-02/421-010-CasesInNotFullyVaccinated.pdf

4   Bartholomew, K. (2021). By design: Aligning values to improve outcomes in a public utility model. *Journal of Public Health International, 4*(3), 15–21.

Chapter 25

1   National Council of State Boards of Nursing. (2023). NCSBN research projects significant nursing workforce shortages and crisis. NCSBN. https://www.ncsbn.org/news/ncsbn-research-projects-significant-nursing-workforce-shortages-and-crisis

2   American Association of Colleges of Nursing. (2022). Fact sheet: Nursing faculty shortage. AACN. https://www.aacnnursing.org/Portals/0/PDFs/Fact-Sheets/Faculty-Shortage-Factsheet.pdf.

3   Cherry, K. (2023). How to increase your sense of belonging. *Verywell Mind.* https://www.verywellmind.com/what-is-the-need-to-belong-2795393

4   Press Ganey. (2016). Nursing special report: The role of workplace safety and surveillance capacity in driving nurse and patient outcomes. Press Ganey.

5   Stimpfel, A. W., Sloane, D. M., & Aiken, L. H. (2012). The longer the shifts for hospital nurses, the higher the levels of burnout and patient dissatisfaction. *Health affairs (Project Hope), 31*(11), 2501–2509. https://doi.org/10.1377/hlthaff.2011.1377

Contributors

We are grateful for our authors, those on the front line, in the class-room, and beyond. They speak from the heart, they speak from personal experience, and their words are bold!

A special thank you to Bernadette M. Melnyk for a profound Foreword, and to Katie Boston-Leary for a transformative second Foreword. We value and appreciate you and your commitment to this process.

To the team of contributors, a warm thank you. We could not have created this collaborative work, nor could we share this information globally, without your support. Allow us to introduce these excep-tional professionals—please meet them now!

Workforce

Nikki Akparewa, RN, MSN, MPH

Health Equity Education Coach, Nurse Entrepreneur/Influencer

Nikki is the founder of Transform Nursing. With almost twenty years of experience in coaching, leading, and developing nurses, her focus is on equipping nurses with inclusive leadership skills by providing them with the tools to confidently address health inequities. She is an author and visionary. Nikki is a graduate of the University of Washington as well as Johns Hopkins University School of Nursing and Public Health. She is currently a clinical instructor at the University of Maryland School of Nursing.

Benjamin Joel Breboneria, DNS, MA, MSN, RN, CNE, NEA-BC

Global Health Leader, Commissioner/NLN, Academic Program Director

"Benjo," as his close friends and colleagues call him, has been exposed to the extensive yet fulfilling landscape of nursing education and leadership. He is passionate about empowering others, utilizing the power of his voice to give opportunities for others to speak for themselves. He's an eloquent leader and a competent team player who exuberates an unbridled passion for learning. President-elect of Sigma's Phi Gamma chapter, he is a graduate of St. Paul University in the Philippines.

Byron Carlisle, MSN, RN, CCRN-K, SCRN

Director of Neuroscience Services for UT Southwestern Medical Center

Byron received his undergraduate BSN from the University of Missouri–Columbia, Sinclair School of Nursing (2009) and MSN,

Administration from the University of Texas–Tyler (2022). A published author and accomplished speaker, his passion since embarking on his leadership journey has been nurse retention and nurse staffing ratios. He is a member of the American Association of Critical Care Nurses, the American Association of Neuroscience Nurses, and the Texas Organization of Nurse Executives.

Bob Dent, DNP, MBA, RN, NEA-BC, CENP, FACHE, FAAN, FAONL

Vice President, Patient Care and Chief Nursing Officer, Entrepreneur

Bob maintains academic appointments with Emory University, Texas Tech University Health Sciences Center, and the University of Texas of the Permian Basin. Past president of the American Organization for Nursing Leadership, his career spans more than three decades in business and operational roles. He recently launched Dr. Bob Dent LLC, providing executive coaching, consulting, and advising. A renowned professional, award winner, and visionary, Bob is a prolific author of book chapters, journal articles, four books, and presentations related to leadership, culture, improving workplace environments, interprofessional collaboration, and nurse staffing.

Brent Dunworth, DNP, MBA, MSN, BSN, APRN, CRNA, NEA-BC, FAANA

Academic and Healthcare Leader, Speaker

Dr. Brent Dunworth holds a trio of degrees from the University of Pittsburgh, including a BSN, MSN, and DNP. He also holds an MBA from Waynesburg University. Associate nurse executive for advanced practice professionals at Vanderbilt University Medical Center and an assistant professor at Vanderbilt University, Brent has received several prestigious accolades and serves as a national speaker on a range of subjects related to nurse anesthesia and executive leadership, all the while continuing to engage in anesthesiology clinical practice at Vanderbilt.

Nicole George, PhD, MSN, RN, NEA-BC

Military Spouse, Mom, Nurse Leader, Nursing Excellence Promoter

Director of the Nursing Center of Excellence at Press Ganey, Nicole is responsible for driving and implementing strategies aimed at supporting nursing clients across the globe. She previously served as the assistant director of operations at the Magnet Recognition Program, where she managed day-to-day operations and had the privilege of collaborating with exceptional healthcare organizations worldwide. She is currently finishing her PhD in nursing at the University of Texas–Medical Branch, where her focus is centered on the experiences of millennial nurse leaders in acute care.

Tim Raderstorf, DNP, MSN, BS, RN

Trailblazing Healthcare Innovator and Author

The first nurse to hold the chief innovation officer title in academia, Tim empowers frontline healthcare professionals to spark transformative change. His groundbreaking Innovation Studio democratizes innovation, providing interprofessional teams with funding, tools, and mentorship to turn ideas into action. Tim coauthored (with Bernadette Melnyk) the #1 new release and book of the year *Evidence-Based Leadership, Innovation and Entrepreneurship in Nursing and Healthcare: A Practical Guide for Success*. Tim's accolades also include the Innovation Studio being named Non-Profit of the Year by *Columbus Business First*.

Joe Tye, MBA, MHA, BA

Author, Speaker, Consultant

The renowned founder of Values Coach, Joe is best known for his work in positive cultures of ownership. He created the Twelve Core Action Values, a sixty-module course on values-based life and leadership skills. In some circles he is best known for "The Pickle Challenge" for a more positive workplace environment, and for the catchphrase "proceed until apprehended" from *The Florence Prescription*. Joe earned an MHA from the University of Iowa and an MBA from the Stanford Graduate School of Business.

Enoh Ukpong, PhD, MSN, RN

Academic, Author

Enoh is a CPR Instructor, Nurse, Midwife and Educator. She earned her bachelor's and master's degrees at Anna Maria College in Paxton, Massachusetts, and her terminal degree from Columbia Pacific University. Her self-published autobiography, titled *Joy Comes in the Morning: The Power of Drive, Discipline, and Determination*, is available on Amazon in paperback and on Kindle as an eBook.

Well-Being

Bonnie and Mark Barnes

Cofounders, The DAISY Foundation

Bonnie and Mark Barnes are renowned in healthcare circles. They were retired when Mark's son Patrick, age thirty-three, developed the autoimmune disease ITP and died after eight weeks in the hospital.

Pat's death was a terrible surprise to his family. However, the nursing care they experienced compelled them to express their gratitude to nurses everywhere for the clinical skill and especially the compassionate care nurses provide every day. This is why the Barneses created the DAISY Foundation (an acronym for diseases attacking the immune system) and the DAISY Award for Extraordinary Nurses.

Today, the DAISY Award is celebrated in over six thousand healthcare facilities and nursing schools in thirty-nine countries. The DAISY Award provides healthcare leaders the means to highlight all the "right" going on in their organizations, providing great role-modeling opportunities and a way to make tangible the organizations' mission and values.

Katie Boston-Leary, PhD, MBA, MHA, RN, NEA-BC

Healthcare Leader, Adjunct Professor, Speaker

Director of nursing programs at the American Nurses Association, Katie oversees the Nursing Practice and Work Environment division and Healthy Nurse, Healthy Nation. She is also co-lead for Project Firstline, a multimillion-dollar grant collaborative with the Centers for Disease Control and Prevention. Cochair of the diversity, equity, and inclusion committee of the Healthcare Leadership Network of the Delaware Valley, an ACHE chapter, she completed her doctorate in health services at Walden University, obtained an MBA/MHA from the University of Maryland Global Campus, and earned her BSN from Bowie State University in Maryland.

Sheila Anne Burke, DNP, MBA, MSN, RN

Former Strategic Nurse Leader, Compliance and Accreditation Consultant

Sheila Anne Burke sadly passed away before the publication of this book on March 30, 2024. A nurse executive with more than two decades of experience in leading nursing education programs from concept to application and through accreditation, she held leadership roles in healthcare administration as well as nursing education. She created and collaborated on programs to improve student engagement and the development of innovative clinical education affiliations. She mentored nursing deans and faculty to achieve advanced leadership skills.

Anna Dermenchyan, PhD, RN, CCRN-K, CPHQ

Nurse leader who cultivates strong relationships to perform meaningful work

Interim chief quality officer of the UCLA Department of Medicine, Anna oversees quality activities that improve the quality of care and designs and implements interventions that improve population health. Her expertise includes bioethics, critical care, quality and patient safety, organizational leadership, performance and process improvement, and health data analytics. An author and speaker, she has served as a Jonas Policy scholar with the American Academy of Nursing and a health policy and media fellow with the George Washington University Center for Health Policy and Media Engagement.

Vicki Good, DNP, RN, CPPS, CENP

Nurse Leader, Professional Society Executive, Advocate

Vicki Good has been a leader in critical care, patient safety, and education. She writes, presents, and serves as a subject matter expert on a variety of healthcare topics, and serves in professional organizations to advance the nursing profession, including the Nurse Staffing Think Tank and Taskforce. She is a past president of the American Association of Critical Care Nurses (AACN) and a lifetime member. She was recently appointed chief clinical officer.

Sue Johnson, PhD, RN, NE-BC, NPD-BC, FAAN

Nurse Author and Advocate

Sue Johnson is a nursing professional development consultant and speaker who provides resource support to clinical educators in multiple settings. Founder and principal of RN Innovations LLC, she speaks to the accomplishments of Nightingale and early nurse leaders. Sue holds a PhD in health administration, dual certifications in nursing professional development and as a nurse executive and is a fellow of the American Academy of Nursing. Sue is a mentor, peer reviewer, and leader who encourages nurses to succeed personally and professionally.

Anne Llewellyn, MS, BCPA, RN, CMGT-BC, CRRN, FCM

Nurse Advocate, Digital Journalist

Anne has been a leader in case management and was the president of the Case Management Society of America from 2003–2004. Awarded the organization's Lifetime Achievement Award in 2015, she is a founding member of the Patient Advocate Certification Board and developed and launched the first National Certification in Patient Advocacy in 2012.

Bernadette M. Melnyk, PhD, APRN-CNP, EBP-C, FAANP, FAAN

Core2Thrive Creator/Founder, Educator, Chief Wellness Officer

Nationally and globally renowned for her clinical knowledge and her innovative approaches to a wide range of healthcare challenges, Bernadette was the first chief wellness officer in the country at The Ohio State University. Her groundbreaking work spans evidence-based practice, intervention research, child and adolescent mental health, and health and wellness. A frequent keynote speaker at national and international conferences, she has consulted with hundreds of healthcare systems and colleges worldwide on improving quality of care and patient outcomes by implementing and sustaining evidence-based practice. She is the foremost authority on wellness and evidence-based practice.

Megan Amaya, PhD, CHES, NBC-HWC

Health and Wellness Advocate, Educator, Author

Associate clinical professor and director of health promotion and wellness at The Ohio State University College of Nursing, Megan leads a team that implements wellness strategy, programs, and services for university students, faculty, staff, and the state of Ohio community. Megan is principal investigator on multiple health and wellness research projects. President-elect for the National Consortium for Building Healthy Academic Communities and member of several university and college of nursing committees, she is a certified health education specialist and board-certified health and wellness coach.

Ian Saludares, MPA, BSN, RN, NEA-BC, CPXP

Lifelong Learner, Healthcare Leader, Mentor

Originally from the Philippines, Ian moved to New York in 1999 and has since held pivotal roles at New York Presbyterian Westchester and Northwell Lenox Hill Hospital, focusing on critical care and patient experience. His active participation in professional organizations like the Beryl Institute, American College of Healthcare Executives, and American Association for Men in Nursing (AAMN) highlights his commitment to advancing the field. Recognized for his leadership and excellence, Ian has received numerous awards, including the Distinction in Leadership Award from Northwell Lenox Hill Hospital and the Nurse Leader Excellence Award from New York Presbyterian.

Wisdom

Kathleen Bartholomew, MSN, RN

Author, Health Culture Expert

An international keynote speaker and culture expert for over twenty years, Kathleen uses the power of story and her strong background in sociology to help leaders create a culture of trust. Her TEDx talk challenges our covert belief that some people are more important than others. Kathleen has published numerous articles and authored *Speak Your Truth: Proven Strategies for Effective Nurse-Physician Communication*, *Ending Nurse-to-Nurse Hostility*, and coauthored *Charting the Course* and *The Dauntless Nurse: Communication Confidence Builder*.

Melissa Burdi, DNP, MSN, BSN

Dean, Executive, Six Sigma

Vice president and dean of the Purdue Global School of Nursing, Melissa is an experienced executive in higher education and has led major service lines in the patient care setting in various metropolitan healthcare systems. Her areas of expertise include establishing strategic partnerships, increasing quality, safety, and high reliability in acute care, process improvement, leadership development, and cardiac care. In 2019, she was appointed as a nursing fellow with the American Association of Colleges of Nursing (AACN).

Cathy Catrambone, PhD, RN, FAAN

Global Nurse Leader, Professional Governance Leader, Policy and Advocacy Activist

Associate professor and associate chairperson in adult health and gerontological nursing at Rush University College of Nursing, Cathy served as president of Sigma Theta Tau International (Sigma) from 2015–2017. She was a leader in Sigma's Global Advisory Panel for the Future of Nursing and Midwifery (GAPFON) that focused on establishing a voice and vision for the future of nursing and midwifery that will advance global health and strengthen professional roles. Her clinical background is adult pulmonary critical care.

Christina Dempsey, DNP, MSN, MBA, CNOR, CENP, FAAN

Consultant, Global Healthcare Leader, Author

CEO of Christina Dempsey Enterprises LLC and the former chief nursing officer for Press Ganey Associates, Dempsey has over three decades of healthcare experience and has served as adjunct faculty for the Missouri State University School of Nursing. A fellow in the American Academy of Nursing, and president of the Missouri Organization of Nurse Leaders, the Nightingale College Board of Managers, the board of Magnit LLC (a global workforce management company), and the board of Children's Mercy Hospital Kansas City, she is an advocate and spokesperson for nurses and nursing.

Jacqueline Dunbar-Jacob, PhD, RN, FAAN

Dean Emeritus, Distinguished Service Professor of Nursing, Author

Dean of the School of Nursing at the University of Pittsburgh from 2001–2022, Jacqueline is an advisory professor at the University of Fudan in Shanghai, China, honorary professor of nursing at Capital

Medical University in Beijing, and visiting professor in nursing at Taipei Medical University in Taipei, Taiwan. She is an accomplished scholar and both a registered nurse (RN) and licensed psychologist.

Kim Evans, APRN, CNS-BC, AHN-BC, CNAT
CEO, Entrepreneur, Holistic Practitioner

As owner of the Institute for Integrative Medicine, Kim is an advanced practice nurse with a passion for helping others achieve their best health—body, mind, and spirit. She recognized early in her career that 75 percent of patients had illnesses that could have been prevented, so she dedicated herself to stopping preventable diseases. Author of *Transforming Healthcare: Healing You, Me and our Broken Disease-Care System*, Kim practices what she preaches by eating healthy, exercising regularly, and meditating/praying daily.

Alina Kushkyan, MD, PhD
Dean, Influencer, Researcher, Consultant, Change-Maker

For over three decades, Alina has led the field in healthcare and academic spaces. She has served as director of Yerevan State Armenian American Medical College "Erebouni" in Armenia, actively contributing to nursing education, academic research, community development, lecturing, and healthcare management. Alina played a critical role in reforming nursing and nursing education in Armenia, pioneering the creation of the country's first three-year nursing program and four-year baccalaureate degree in nursing (BSN) in collaboration with the University of California of Los Angeles, supported by AIHA/USAID. She was instrumental in establishing the Armenian Nurses Association in 1995.

About the Authors

Sharon M. Weinstein, MS, RN, CRNI-R®, CSP®, FACW, FAAN

Certified Speaking Professional (CSP), Author, Innovator, Design Thinker

Sharon brings an impressive four decades of senior executive, clinical, and academic experience to the forefront. As the coauthor with Dina Readinger of *Think Differently: 18 Strategies to Fix Broken Thinking*, she has written twenty-two books and over 160 peer-reviewed manuscripts. A TEDx Montreal Women presenter, Sharon is also a fellow of the American Academy of Nursing. Her extensive work has transcended borders, fostering inclusive cultures of collaboration in the public and private sectors, both nationally and internationally. Her body of work reflects a lifelong commitment to partnering with organizations that want to create a strong workforce, boost workplace engagement, and prioritize staff well-being. Sharon operates as a partner in Design Think LLC.

Dina Readinger, BS, EMBA

Leadership Development and Team Optimization Coach

With a career spanning four decades in healthcare, pharmaceutical, and biotech, Dina Readinger has emerged as a pioneering force behind the creation of Diagnostic Design Thinking. Following her exit from the corporate world in 2015, she has coached hundreds of women executives around the world, introducing them to innovative leadership strategies grounded in Diagnostic Design Thinking. Dina collaborates with CEOs, CFOs, COOs, and HR directors, providing expertise in retention strategies, leadership development, and team performance optimization. Beyond her coaching role, Dina is a distinguished speaker, consultant, certified coach, franchise owner, and coauthor with Sharon Weinstein of *Think Differently: 18 Strategies to Fix Broken Thinking*. Dina operates as a partner in Design Think LLC.